Crime Scene Processing and Laboratory Workbook

**Patrick Jones
Ralph E. Williams**

CRC Press
Taylor & Francis Group
Boca Raton   London   New York

CRC Press is an imprint of the
Taylor & Francis Group, an **informa** business

CRC Press
Taylor & Francis Group
6000 Broken Sound Parkway NW, Suite 300
Boca Raton, FL 33487-2742

Library of Congress Cataloging-in-Publication Data

Jones, Patrick, 1946-
  Crime scene processing and laboratory workbook / authors, Patrick Jones, Ralph E. Williams.
    p. cm.
  Includes bibliographical references and index.
  ISBN 978-1-4200-8542-6 (hardcover : alk. paper)
  1. Crime scene searches. 2. Crime laboratories. 3. Criminal investigation. 4. Evidence, Criminal. I. Williams, Ralph E. II. Title.

HV8073.J62 2009
363.25--dc22   2008054118

Visit the Taylor & Francis Web site at
http://www.taylorandfrancis.com

and the CRC Press Web site at
http://www.crcpress.com

Crime
Proce
and
Labo
Work

Dedication

To all the CSIs, detectives, investigators, evidence technicians, criminalists, lab analysts, and police officers who daily do their job to enable justice, and to those who will follow in our footsteps—the next generation.

Epigraph

Tell me and I forget . . .
Show me and I learn . . .
Involve me and I understand.

—Confucius

Contents

Preface

Welcome to the wonderful world of forensic science and the crime scene investigator (CSI). First, it must be understood that being a CSI is neither glamorous, exciting, nor flashy. Being a CSI is not like it is depicted on TV. There are no backlit labs with 4-feet by 8-feet light tables. CSIs do not chase criminals. They do not make arrests, nor do they get into gunfights. They do not interview witnesses or interrogate suspects. They do process the crime scene. They do collect and "bag and tag" evidence. They document the crime scene with photo images, measurements, drawings, and reports. They write detailed, unbiased technical reports. Lots and lots of reports!

CSIs are specialists. They are *objective* investigators. The objective investigator deals with physical facts (evidence). If something can be felt, seen, smelled, or heard (not tasted—we never "taste" anything), it is the CSI's job to collect and document it. The most important part of the job is documentation. Forensic is defined "as pertains to a court of law." Documentation is what "tells the story." Documentation is what shows the story (photo images). Documentation is what proves a suspect guilty or innocent.

Crime Scene Processing and Laboratory Workbook encompasses an array of exercises to assist students in learning the techniques of collection and processing of physical evidence. These exercises are designed for hands-on learning and require using the actual tools and proper procedures for crime scene processing and evidence collection as followed in today's crime scene investigative industry. The exercises are designed for both individual and team participation. Included in this workbook are all the forms needed for each exercise, along with instructions outlining the proper procedures in using the report forms.

The exercises cover a broad selection of forensic crime scene procedures, including documentation techniques and photo imaging, specific techniques of fingerprint recovery, blood evidence collection and processing, impression and toolmark recovery and preservation, firearm recovery, car crash procedures, and collection, processing, and interpretation of soil and entomological evidence.

The Authors

Patrick Jones is currently the forensic lab director, forensic science coordinator, and a graduate faculty member at Purdue University. He teaches graduate courses in forensic lasers and alternate light sources, and forensic digital imaging, as well as undergraduate courses in crime scene investigation, forensic digital imaging, evidence collection techniques, and scene documentation. He is currently conducting research with forensic lasers and alternate light sources. He is a deputy coroner and certified medico-legal death investigator with the White County, Indiana, Coroner's Office. He is a retired Cook County (Illinois) sheriff's police investigator with 21 years of service. His service assignments include 15 years as a crime scene investigator (CSI). He has a BS degree from Pacific Western University and an MS degree from LaSalle University. He is a graduate of a National Law Enforcement Academy (DEA). He is a member of the board of directors of the International Association for Identification, Indiana Division, the American Academy for Forensic Science, the International Association of Homicide Investigators, the Indiana Association of Homicide and Violent Crimes Investigator Association, the Indiana Physics Association, the Indiana Microscopy Society, and the Indiana Coroner's Association.

Ralph E. Williams, PhD, D-ABFE, is a professor of entomology at Purdue University and the director of the Purdue Forensic Science Program. He teaches courses in forensic science and forensic entomology and taphonomy. He is doing research in forensic entomology, working with several graduate and undergraduate students. Dr. Williams has a BS degree from Purdue University, an MS degree from Virginia Tech University, and a PhD degree from Oklahoma State University. He has served on the Purdue University faculty since 1976. He is board certified by and a diplomate of the American Board of Forensic Entomologists (ABFE). He also holds memberships in the North American Forensic Entomology Association, American Academy of Forensic Sciences, Indiana Homicide & Violent Crime Investigators Association, Indiana Coroner's Association, and is a deputy coroner in White County, Indiana. Dr. Williams has authored more than 35 scientific publications, authored and/or co-authored four books, and has made more than 100 presentations at scientific meetings. He has had extensive experience dealing with legal matters associated with insect nuisance associated with confined livestock and poultry, pests of public health concern, and forensic entomology death investigation and medico-legal concerns.

Equipment and Camera

Goal: The goal of this exercise is to examine, become familiar with, and learn how to use the camera and basic equipment of the CSI, crime scene investigator.

In this exercise you will work alone, without a partner.

Exercise Part A

1. Examine your equipment.
2. Become familiar with it.
3. You are responsible for maintaining and stocking your evidence kit.
4. Remember to have extra batteries in the evidence kit.
5. Case contents:
   - Case—hard or soft-sided
   - Magnifying glass
   - Tape: clear, plastic, approximately 1.88" × 22 yards
   - Flashlight, with extra batteries
   - Tape measure: 25 feet
   - Tweezers/forceps
   - Small knife
   - Evidence envelopes, 3.5" × 5" (10)
   - Evidence bags, small (10)
   - Evidence bags, medium (10)
   - Black fingerprint powder (1/2 ounce)
   - Silver fingerprint powder (1/2 ounce)
   - Black magnetic powder (1/2 ounce)
   - Latent fingerprint brushes (2)
   - Cotton tip applicators (single cotton tip)
   - Graph paper, ¼-inch squares
   - Dry erase marker (black)
   - Sharpie permanent marker
   - Pen (black ink)
   - Pencil, #2 (mechanical)
   - 12-inch ruler
   - Notebook

The following items are listed in the appendices:
- Photo ID Card, Appendix E (This should be the first photo image taken for each case. Used to identify photo images. This card should be laminated. A dry erase marker should be used to mark the card, allowing the card to be used over and over.)
- Scales, Appendix C
- Tent Cards, Appendix D

Exercise Part B

Examine the digital camera.

1. Become familiar with how to turn it on.
2. Become familiar with its settings.
3. Learn how to transfer images to a computer.
4. Learn how to print those images (see Appendix D).
5. Learn and remember the minimum focus of your camera. The following is a method to determine your minimum focus. After you determine it by this method, check your camera's manual to see how close you are to the camera manual.
    a. Place the photo ID card on the floor.
    b. Turn the flash on.
    c. At a distance of about 48" from the ID card, take the first image. Is it in focus? If yes, move 6" closer.
    d. Take another image, this time at 42". Is it in focus? If yes, move 6" closer.
    e. Take another image. If it is in focus, move 6" closer.
    f. Take another. Is it in focus? If yes, move 6" closer.
    g. Keep doing this until the image is out of focus.
    h. The range between in-focus and out-of-focus is your minimum focus.
    i. Now, write your minimum focus below.
       Minimum focus: _____ inches

Do not hand this page in. Keep it. It is for your information.

6. Now, practice taking some images.
    a. The first image you always take should be the ID card. Take this image close up, so that you can read everything on the card.
    b. The second will be a photo image of an "N." This is the North image. Take it so that a good deal of the background shows in the image. This allows you to acclimate yourself to the images months and sometimes years after the images are taken, i.e., when you go to court.
7. Take images of small items both with and without scale.
8. Take each item with flash and with ambient light (available light).
9. Out-of-focus or bad images may not be erased. Treat them just as though they were real crime scene photo images.

10. Use the provided sheet to record the images. Check the column "Amb." for ambient light or "Flash" for flash. Indicate with or without scale in the "Special Lighting, Tool, or Technique" column.

11. Photo image the following items:

    a. A car (four sides). You do not need a scale for this. We use the scale for relatively small items.

    b. A person: front, back, and ID (face).

    c. A soft drink can (don't forget a scale).

    d. A book, closed and open (don't forget a scale).

    e. When you print your images, they do not have to be 8″ × 10″ images. See Appendix F "How to print small images."

Notes

Chapter

Report Writing and Crime Scene Documentation

Goal: The goal of this exercise is to practice and learn the proper method of documenting a crime scene using report forms. Forms and other documentation are the uninteresting part of a CSI's work, but it is one of the most important parts of any investigation. If the case, evidence, and scene are not correctly and precisely documented, the case cannot go to court successfully, and a guilty person may be set free.

In this exercise you will work without a partner.

The Scenario

There has been a burglary at the Burger King located at 3993 W. Torch Street, Yourtown, Indiana. The burglary was discovered by the manager, Ben Bear, at 0600 hours on June 1, 2008. When he arrived at work he noticed the rear door had been pried open. There was a crowbar on the ground next to the door. He then called 911, and Officer Smith arrived and took the original report. The weather is cool, 64°F with a light rain. Dispatch has assigned you to the burglary. You are to meet Officer Smith at the scene. He has secured the scene and is standing by waiting for you. Upon arrival, Officer Smith advises you that the rear door had been pried open to gain entry. The money is kept in a safe, but the perpetrators did not try to open it. Some damage was done in the counter area. Some food is missing but, as far as the manager can tell, nothing else is missing.

Write a report based on the information above. "Collect" any important evidence. "Take photo images" of whatever is important. (Note: The evidence you collect and the photo images that you take are imaginary.) List them, describe them, and explain the method used to collect and package the evidence. List the photo images that you would have taken as if the scene actually existed. Write neatly or print. Remember that the report will be read by your CSI supervisor, the head of detectives (before it is assigned), and by the lead investigator.

- The case number is 0000-002
- The inventory control number is I-0000-002

The reports you will need for this case are:

1. Crime scene investigator's report
2. Inventory sheet (if evidence is collected)
3. Laboratory submission request (if evidence is to be submitted to the lab for analysis)

If you have questions about completing the report, remember to refer to the report form instructions in Appendix A.

Crime Scene
Investigator's Report

Report Classification [   ]   Case Number [   ]

Date/Time [   ]   Type of Location [   ]   Agency [   ]   Investigator [   ]

Victim's Name [   ]   Victim's Address [   ]

Injuries [   ]   Taken for Treatment [   ]   Victim Rape Kit [   ]   Suspect in Custody [   ]

Suspect Rape Kit [   ]   Weapon [   ]   Gunshot Residue [   ]   Gun Sheet [   ]

Weather [   ]   Inside Temperature [   ]   Outside Temperature [   ]   Crime Scene Drawing [   ]

Alcohol [   ]   Drugs [   ]   Lighting Conditions [   ]

Vehicle [   ]   Make [   ]   Model [   ]   Year [   ]   Color [   ]

Vehicle Sheet [   ]   License Plate [   ]   License Plate State [   ]

Other Distinguishing Characteristics [   ]

Inventory Control Number [   ]   Images Taken [   ]

Evidence Collected				**Photo Images**		
1		23		1		23
2		24		2		24
3		25		3		25
4		26		4		26
5		27		5		27
6		28		6		28
7		29		7		29
8		30		8		30
9		31		9		31
10		32		10		32
11		33		11		33
12		34		12		34
13		35		13		35
14		36		14		36
15		37		15		37
16		38		16		38
17		39		17		39
18		40		18		40
19		41		19		41
20		42		20		42
21		43		21		43
22		44		22		44

Note: Start listing photo images on this report - if additional space is needed use photo image continuation report.

Signature [   ]   Page [   ]

Narrative:

Signature	Supervisor's Signature	Page

Inventory Sheet

Case Number [ ]

Date/Time [ ]   Agency [ ]   Investigator [ ]

Type of Case [ ]   Inventory Control Number [ ]

Item No.	Quantity	Description of Items

Note: Item numbers above should be the same as those on the report form. Items recovered from separate locations or recovered under a different case number should be listed on separate lab submission sheets.
Describe below pertinent information that could help in examination or testing (required).

Case Info

Submitting Officer   Date/Time

Signature   Page

Laboratory Submission
Request

Report Classification [   ]   Case Number [   ]

Date/Time [   ]   Agency [   ]   Investigator [   ]

Victim's Name [   ]   Victim's Address [   ]

Type of Case [   ]   Inventory Control Number [   ]

Item No.	Description of Item	Type of Test or Examination Requested	Returned to Agency Date

Note: Item numbers above should be the same as those on the report form and the inventory form. Items from separate locations or recovered under a different case number should be listed on separate lab submission sheets. Describe below pertinent information that could help in examination or testing (required).

Case Info

Submitting Officer	Lab Person Receiving	Date/Time
Signature	Signature	Page

Notes

Chapter

The Crime Scene

Goal: The goal of this exercise is to process a minor crime scene, document it, and collect evidence. Evidence must be photo imaged and properly packaged either for analysis or for storing in the evidence room as evidence—not analyzed. Not all items of evidence require analysis, but some do require being kept secured and with a documented chain of custody. An example is a baby bassinet (small tub used to bathe small babies). If there was a drowning, the prosecutor might want to show the tub to the jury for impact, but there is no analysis of the bassinet by the crime lab.

In this exercise you will work without a partner.

The Scenario

Dispatch has assigned you to the scene of a robbery at 1908 S. Homan, Apt. 3-F, Yourtown, IL. As it turns out, it is a burglary. (The difference is that there is no one at home during a burglary. If someone is home, it is a robbery. Burglary is "crime vs. property" and robbery is "crime vs. persons.") Mr. Roboto is the victim.

A uniformed officer is at the scene awaiting your arrival. Officer Smith, the uniformed officer, is at the door with a crime scene entry log. (Crime scene entry logs are normally not used on simple burglaries, but there is nothing prohibiting this. Using one in this case will give you additional practice.) As a CSI, process the scene using your residence (just one or two rooms) for your "scene."

1. Prepare a CSI case report.
    a. The case number is 0000-003.
    b. Complete and fill in all fields. Do not leave any fields blank.
    c. Complete a narrative—it should begin as explained in the report instructions in Appendix A. Remember: Who, what, when, where, how, and why should be answered in the narrative.
        i. Information requested:
        ii. UNK—if the information exists but you do not know it
        iii. NA—if the information does not exist (in this space-time continuum)
        iv. NONE—if the box requires a numerical answer and there is none
2. The inventory control number is I-0000-003.
3. Prepare a crime scene entry log. (Remember: You are never the first one on the sheet. The uniformed officer standing security at the scene is first. In this case, Officer Smith has already started a log.) While the scene is being processed, you and everyone entering and leaving the scene must sign in and out.
4. Photo image the scene. List images on the report. If there are more images than will fit on the report, use a photo image continuation report. The images are always started on the main case report and the overflow is continued on the photo image continuation report.

13

LIVERPOOL JOHN MOORES UNIVERSITY
LEARNING SERVICES

5. Print the pictures.
6. Collect at least two pieces of evidence.
   a. The evidence should be simple and not valuable.
   b. Complete an inventory sheet.
7. If any of the evidence should be examined at the lab, an evidence submission form must be completed. Make your requests realistic. For example, for the burglary in question, do not ask to have five items tested for DNA.

The following forms are needed:

1. Crime scene entry log
2. Crime scene investigator's report
3. Evidence continuation report, if more items are collected than will fit on the case report.
4. Photo image continuation report, if more photo images are taken than will fit on the case report.
5. Inventory sheet
6. Laboratory submission request, if the evidence will be submitted to the lab for analysis.

Additional Note: These reports require time, effort, and careful attention to detail. Do not just jot something down. Write the reports as though they may be read by the Supreme Court of the United States of America, *because they may be.*

Crime Scene
Investigator's Report

Report Classification [   ]   Case Number [   ]

Date/Time [   ]   Type of Location [   ]   Agency [   ]   Investigator [   ]

Victim's Name [   ]   Victim's Address [   ]

Injuries [   ]   Taken for Treatment [   ]   Victim Rape Kit [   ]   Suspect in Custody [   ]

Suspect Rape Kit [   ]   Weapon [   ]   Gunshot Residue [   ]   Gun Sheet [   ]

Weather [   ]   Inside Temperature [   ]   Outside Temperature [   ]   Crime Scene Drawing [   ]

Alcohol [   ]   Drugs [   ]   Lighting Conditions [   ]

Vehicle [   ]   Make [   ]   Model [   ]   Year [   ]   Color [   ]

Vehicle Sheet [   ]   License Plate [   ]   License Plate State [   ]

Other Distinguishing Characteristics [   ]

Inventory Control Number [   ]   Images Taken [   ]

Evidence Collected				Photo Images			
1		23		1		23	
2		24		2		24	
3		25		3		25	
4		26		4		26	
5		27		5		27	
6		28		6		28	
7		29		7		29	
8		30		8		30	
9		31		9		31	
10		32		10		32	
11		33		11		33	
12		34		12		34	
13		35		13		35	
14		36		14		36	
15		37		15		37	
16		38		16		38	
17		39		17		39	
18		40		18		40	
19		41		19		41	
20		42		20		42	
21		43		21		43	
22		44		22		44	

Note: Start listing photo images on this report - if additional space is needed use photo image continuation report.

Signature [   ]

Page [   ]

Narrative:

| Signature | Supervisor's Signature | Page |

Crime Scene
Entry Log

Report Classification [   ]   Case Number [   ]

Location/Description [   ]

Type of Location [   ]   Agency [   ]   Log Officer [   ]

All persons entering this crime scene will sign in and out and state their purpose for entering.

Name & Title	Date/Time In	Date/Time Out	Reason for Entering

Signature of Log Officer

This report should not be typed. All entries
should be made by hand in black ink.   Page [   ]

Inventory Sheet

Case Number [   ]

Date/Time [   ]   Agency [   ]   Investigator [   ]

Type of Case [   ]   Inventory Control Number [   ]

Item No.	Quantity	Description of Items

Note: Item numbers above should be the same as those on the report form. Items recovered from separate locations or recovered under a different case number should be listed on separate lab submission sheets.
Describe below pertinent information that could help in examination or testing (required).

Case Info

Submitting Officer	Date/Time
Signature	Page

Evidence Continuation Report

Report Classification		Case Number	

Date/Time		Type of Location		Agency		Investigator	

Victim's Name		Victim's Address	

Inventory Control Number	

Item Number	Description of Item

Signature	Supervisor's Signature	Page

Photo Image
Continuation Report

Report Classification [   ]   Case Number [   ]

Date/Time [   ]   Type of Location [   ]   Agency [   ]   Investigator [   ]

Victim's Name [   ]   Victim's Address [   ]

Image Number	Description of Image

Signature	Supervisor's Signature	Page [ ]

Laboratory Submission
Request

Report Classification	Case Number
Date/Time	Agency	Investigator
Victim's Name	Victim's Address
Type of Case	Inventory Control Number

Item No.	Description of Item	Type of Test or Examination Requested	Returned to Agency Date

Note: Item numbers above should be the same as those on the report form and the inventory form. Items from separate locations or recovered under a different case number should be listed on separate lab submission sheets. Describe below pertinent information that could help in examination or testing (required).

Case Info

Submitting Officer	Lab Person Receiving	Date/Time
Signature	Signature	Page

Notes

Chapter 4

Photo Imaging Assignment

Goal: The goal of this exercise is to practice and learn the use of the camera, becoming more familiar with its capabilities and your ability.

In this exercise you will work without a partner.

Report forms and items needed for submission:

1. Photo listing sheets (three), listing the subject matter of the photo image taken. The photo sheet should have a description of each photograph taken. Images should be in focus and viewable. Out-of-focus and badly lit images may be erased or deleted for *this exercise only*. This is not a crime scene, but rather a photo assignment, so the rules that govern crime scenes do not apply to this assignment.

2. Photo images:

Take the following photo images:

Item	Image	Instructions	Number of Photos
1	ID card	Close up	1
2	Can	Top, bottom, back, front, one with scale	5
3	Pencil	Top, bottom, back, front, one with scale	5
4	TV, off	Front	1
5	TV, on	Front	1
6	Knife	Both sides, with and without scale	4
7	Vehicle	4 sides, VIN[a], license plate	6
8	Tire tread	With and without scale	2
9	Artifact	On vehicle (a scratch, dent, sticker), with and without scale	2
10	Cell phone	Both sides, open and shut, on and off, with scale	6
11	Door lock	Striker, striker plate, with and without scale, and door jam	5
12	Food	With and without scale	2
13	Magazine	One page, with and without scale	2
14	Thermostat	With and without scale	2
15	Residence	Where you or your friend lives—must show address	2
16	Street sign	Sign, perspective shot[b]	2
17	Drawer	Open and closed	2
18	Lock	Padlock type, with and without scale	4
19	Face ID	Image of a person, close up, person should take up ¾ of frame	1
20	Tattoo	3, with and without scale	6
21	Body	(May be alive), both sides, face, hands, legs, feet, torso, scars	10+
22	Moving car	3 photo images of moving cars—follow the motion of the car	3

Item	Image	Instructions	Number of Photos
23	Moving person	3 photo images of moving people—follow motion of person	3
24	Shoe	Over all top, bottom, with and without scale	4
25	Item/window	5 photos of items in store window (from outdoors)	5
26	Item/window	5 photos of items in store display window (from indoors)	5

[a] *Vehicle identification number. Located on the driver's side windshield on dash.*
[b] *Perspective shot. Show item of interest in relationship with its surroundings.*

Image Description	Amb.	Flash	Special Lighting, Tool, or Technique

Image Description	Amb.	Flash	Special Lighting, Tool, or Technique

Image Description	Amb.	Flash	Special Lighting, Tool, or Technique

Notes

Chapter  5

Evidence Collecting and Packaging

Goal: The goal of this exercise is to practice and learn the proper method of collecting and packaging evidence.

In this exercise you will work without a partner.

On television we often see CSI and detectives collecting and packaging evidence. But they do it with drama in mind, not the sound evidentiary procedures required for successful court outcomes.

First and foremost: Very little evidence is collected in plastic bags. Plastic looks great and you can see what is on the inside; however, it does not breathe. Consequently, bacteria and mold may form. As an experiment, place a sample of blood from a steak or piece of meat purchased at the grocery store in a plastic bag. Place it somewhere at room temperature, and look at it after about a week. What you see is the same thing that happens to an important swab of blood taken from the crime scene. If it molds or bacteria attack it, the blood swab will be useless when analysis is attempted. When you ask yourself, "Paper or plastic?" say paper.

Plastic is used for a number of items, but never biologicals. You may place a note, paper, or documents in a clear plastic container. When debris is collected from a fire, an unused aluminum can is used. This is done because if it explodes, it will pop the top off and not injure anyone with shrapnel.

When we collect a gun or metal weapon that was found in water, we keep it in an aluminum paint can filled with the same water in which it was found and we keep it in water until we can get it to the lab and to a firearms examiner. We do this because if the gun dries out, it will rust and the firearms examiner will not be able to fire it for testing or ballistics.

Marking and documenting evidence is vitally important. Proper packaging, documentation, and testimony make an item evidence. This is what makes a lead pipe evidence and not just a lead pipe that a police officer found and brought to court.

There are a number of pieces of information that should be included with the evidence in order to document it properly. These include:

- Case number
- Item number
- Inventory control number
- Date and time collected
- The agency's name
- Where the item was collected (address)
- Where the item was collected at the scene (e.g., top of refrigerator in kitchen)
- The name of the person who collected the evidence

The evidence must be sealed. The easiest and most cost-effective method is to use paper bags purchased from a discount warehouse and a pre-inked stamp (Fig. 5.1). Regular clear packaging tape can be used to seal it; however, the preferred method is to use breakaway evidence tape. This tape is very brittle and, if an attempt to remove it is made, it breaks into many pieces. Figure 5.2 shows this type of tape. The bag is folded, and the tape is placed completely across the fold. It is lapped over each side by about an inch and

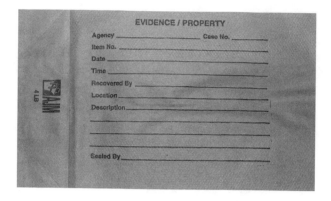

Figure 5.1
This figure shows a plain paper bag that has been stamped with an evidence documentation form.

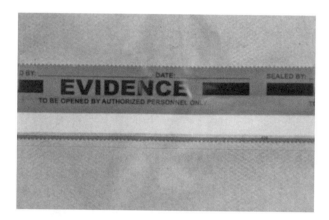

Figure 5.2
The proper method for placing evidence tape on a paper bag containing evidence.

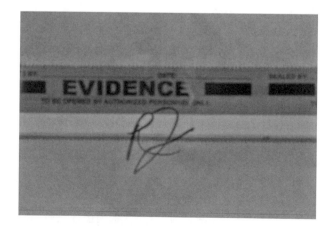

Figure 5.3
The proper method of signing the evidence tape on a paper bag with evidence. Notice that the initials or name are signed over both the paper and the tape.

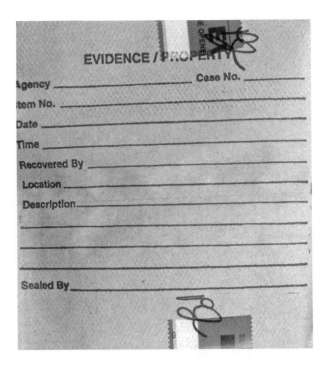

Figure 5.4
The proper method of signing the evidence tape on a paper bag with evidence on the side that the tape laps over the edge. Notice that the initials or name are signed over both the paper and the tape.

secured. The bag is initialed or signed in three (3) places. The first is across the taped fold (Fig. 5.3). The second and third are placed across the tape and paper bag on the reverse side (Fig. 5.4).

The Scenario

Investigator Columbo from your agency, while investigating a case, obtained specific firsthand information concerning a case of unlawful restraint. The information was that the victim, Feona T. Ogre, was given some type of drug by the suspect, P. Fautquat, on November 1st at a party on the third floor of the suspect's building. Fautquat lives at 2223 S. State St., Apt. 3-B, Yourtown, CA. There are 12 apartments in the three-story building.

After Fautquat gave the victim the drug, he took her to his apartment. There he made her write several notes, addressed to him (Fautquat), and possibly took pictures of her—the victim does not have a solid memory of what went on at the apartment. A search warrant was issued by the Circuit Court of Southern California authorizing Detective Columbo and a CSI team to search Fautquat's apartment for notes, pictures, and any other items associated with Feona T. Ogre.

You and Columbo will execute the search warrant on Fautquat and his apartment. You will conduct this search at your residence. Collect, package, document, and photo image the scene. Collect at least six items of evidence. The day that you execute the warrant the weather is sunny and bright with outside temperature of 82°F and an inside temperature of 70°F.

- Case report number is 0000-005
- Inventory control number is I-0000-005

Crime Scene
Investigator's Report

Report Classification [   ]   Case Number [   ]

Date/Time [   ]   Type of Location [   ]   Agency [   ]   Investigator [   ]

Victim's Name [   ]   Victim's Address [   ]

Injuries [   ]   Taken for Treatment [   ]   Victim Rape Kit [   ]   Suspect in Custody [   ]

Suspect Rape Kit [   ]   Weapon [   ]   Gunshot Residue [   ]   Gun Sheet [   ]

Weather [   ]   Inside Temperature [   ]   Outside Temperature [   ]   Crime Scene Drawing [   ]

Alcohol [   ]   Drugs [   ]   Lighting Conditions [   ]

Vehicle [   ]   Make [   ]   Model [   ]   Year [   ]   Color [   ]

Vehicle Sheet [   ]   License Plate [   ]   License Plate State [   ]

Other Distinguishing Characteristics [   ]

Inventory Control Number [   ]   Images Taken [   ]

Evidence Collected				Photo Images			
1		23		1		23	
2		24		2		24	
3		25		3		25	
4		26		4		26	
5		27		5		27	
6		28		6		28	
7		29		7		29	
8		30		8		30	
9		31		9		31	
10		32		10		32	
11		33		11		33	
12		34		12		34	
13		35		13		35	
14		36		14		36	
15		37		15		37	
16		38		16		38	
17		39		17		39	
18		40		18		40	
19		41		19		41	
20		42		20		42	
21		43		21		43	
22		44		22		44	

Note: Start listing photo images on this report - if additional space is needed use photo image continuation report.

Signature [   ]

Page [   ]

Narrative:

Signature	Supervisor's Signature	Page

Inventory Sheet

Case Number

Date/Time   Agency   Investigator

Type of Case   Inventory Control Number

Item No.	Quantity	Description of Items

Note: Item numbers above should be the same as those on the report form and the inventory form. Items recovered from separate locations or recovered under a different case number should be listed on separate lab submission sheets. Describe below pertinent information that could help in examination or testing (required).

Case Info

Submitting Officer   Date/Time

Signature   Page

Laboratory Submission
Request

| Report Classification | | Case Number | |

| Date/Time | | Agency | | Investigator | |

| Victim's Name | | Victim's Address | |

| Type of Case | | Inventory Control Number | |

Item No.	Description of Item	Type of Test or Examination Requested	Returned to Agency Date

Note: Item numbers above should be the same as those on the report form and the inventory form. Items from separate locations or recovered under a different case number should be listed on separate lab submission sheets. Describe below pertinent information that could help in examination or testing (required).

Case Info

Submitting Officer	Lab Person Receiving	Date/Time
Signature	Signature	Page

Notes

Chapter 6

The Secondary Scene

Goal: The goal of this exercise is to process a secondary crime scene. This is a scene that has initially been discovered at another location. The secondary scene can be the main scene. For example, if a gun is found on the corner of 5th and Vine, the CSIs assigned will receive a new case number 0000-0001. A short time later, a body is found at 6th and Vine. It appears they are one and the same case. The body will be given a supplemental case number 0000-0001-A, even though it is the main crime scene. The sequence in which they were discovered determines which are the primary and secondary crime scenes.

In this exercise you will work with a partner or as part of a team.

The Scenario

A death investigation is being conducted by another CSI team. They have been called to 2525 W. State St., Apt. 205, Yourtown, MI. A team of CSIs are processing the scene of a death investigation. (Remember: Even if the victim was shot 16 times by a perpetrator on national television, it is a death investigation, not a homicide, until the coroner or medical examiner declares it to be a homicide.)

The victim is described as a female, white, 25-year-old subject. She was physically identified by a neighbor as the woman living in apartment 205, a Nancy Drew. There was suspect blood found in the apartment. It appears at this time that the victim was stabbed. She had been found by her live-in boyfriend, John Hardy (one of the Hardy Boys); however, after he called the police, he left the scene. Apparently, the boyfriend has a record of drug use. This information is supplied by Detective Columbo.

The only data supplied by the primary team is:

1. Liver mortis is approximately 5%.
2. Rigor mortis is approximately 5%.
3. Algor mortis is 89°F.
4. No weapons were discovered in the apartment.

The apartment building provides a basement storage unit to the renters at this location. Each unit is locked with a simple padlock. Since Drew and Hardy are both on the lease, Detective Columbo, the investigator in charge of the case, has secured a search warrant for the basement storage area. The basement storage unit's physical description is identified as Storage-Basement-205, 2525 W. State St., Yourtown, MI.

You have been assigned to process the secondary scene, the basement storage area. Officer Smith, a uniformed officer, is standing by at the storage room in the basement with the search warrant awaiting your arrival.

The weather outside is 55°F and rainy. Temperature inside is 72°F.

1. Process the scene as a secondary scene (using a crime scene investigator's supplemental report).
2. Photograph and collect any pertinent evidence.
3. Take detailed measurements.
4. Use triangulation to locate objects on your crime scene drawing.*
5. Document the scene with reports, images, and drawings.
6. The case number is 20000-006-A.
7. The inventory control number is I-0000-006-A.
8. Use gloves when recovering evidence.

Report forms you will need:

1. Crime scene entry log
2. Crime scene investigator's supplemental report
3. Photo images
4. Inventory sheet
5. Crime scene drawing (graph paper, ¼-inch squares, blue lines on white paper). Use a ruler to draw straight lines. Make the drawing in pencil. After the drawing is completed, make a photocopy to make it permanent. See the form instructions in Appendix A to learn what is to be placed on the drawing.
6. Laboratory submission request

* The triangulation method of placing items on a drawing.

Triangulation requires the use of two static points. A static point is an item or object that does not move. A table lamp, a couch, or an end table *is not* a static point. The northeast corner of the room, the east side of a door or window, or a fireplace is a static point.

Measurements from two static points are recorded to two separate points on the object in question (Fig. 6.1). When these measurements are taken, by using the same static points to the same two points on the object, the object can be placed back exactly in its original position.

The same technique is used in exterior cases. A static point is not a bush, shrub, or car. A static point is the corner of a building, a telephone pole, or the edge of a paved road (Figs. 6.2 and 6.3).

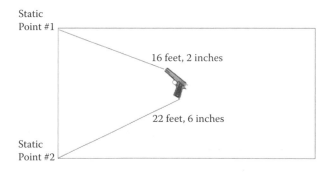

Figure 6.1
An example of triangulation.

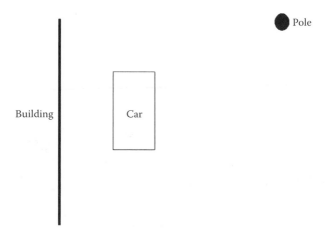

Figure 6.2
A drawing of a vehicle parked near the side of a building and a telephone pole.

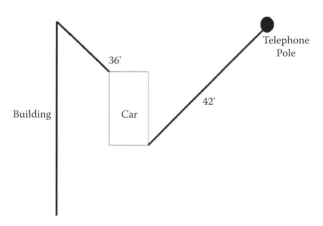

Figure 6.3
A drawing of a vehicle parked near the side of a building and a telephone pole with measurements taken from the telephone pole to the left rear bumper and from the northwest corner of a building to the left front bumper.

Crime Scene Investigator's
Supplemental Report

Report Classification [ ]　　Case Number [ ]

Date/Time [ ]　Type of Location [ ]　Agency [ ]　Investigator [ ]

Victim's Name [ ]　Victim's Address [ ]

Inventory Control Number [ ]　Images Taken [ ]

Evidence Collected　　　　　　**Photo Images**

1		11		1		11	
2		12		2		12	
3		13		3		13	
4		14		4		14	
5		15		5		15	
6		16		6		16	
7		17		7		17	
8		18		8		18	
9		19		9		19	
10		20		10		20	

Narrative:

Signature　　　　　　Supervisor's Signature

Note: Start listing photo images on this report - if additional space is needed use photo image continuation report.　　Page [ ]

Narrative Continued: **Note: Do not print or use this page unless additional space is needed.**

Signature	Supervisor's Signature	Page

Crime Scene
Entry Log

Report Classification			Case Number	
Location/Description				
Type of Location		Agency	Log Officer	

All persons entering this crime scene will sign in and out and state their purpose for entering.

Name & Title	Date/Time In	Date/Time Out	Reason for Entering

Signature of Log Officer

This report should not be typed. All entries
should be made by hand in black ink.

Page

Inventory Sheet

Case Number _____

Date/Time _____ Agency _____ Investigator _____

Type of Case _____ Inventory Control Number _____

Item No.	Quantity	Description of Items

Note: Item numbers above should be the same as those on the report form and the inventory form. Items recovered from separate locations or recovered under a different case number should be listed on separate lab submission sheets. Describe below pertinent information that could help in examination or testing (required).

Case Info

Submitting Officer _____ Date/Time _____

Signature _____ Page _____

Laboratory Submission Request

Report Classification [   ]　　　　Case Number [   ]

Date/Time [   ]　　Agency [   ]　　Investigator [   ]

Victim's Name [   ]　　Victim's Address [   ]

Type of Case [   ]　　Inventory Control Number [   ]

Item No.	Description of Item	Type of Test or Examination Requested	Returned to Agency Date

Note: Item numbers above should be the same as those on the report form and the inventory form. Items from separate locations or recovered under a different case number should be listed on separate lab submission sheets. Describe below pertinent information that could help in examination or testing (required).

Case Info

Submitting Officer	Lab Person Receiving	Date/Time
Signature	Signature	Page

Notes

Chapter 7

Fingerprints

Goal: The goal of this exercise is to practice and learn the basic concepts of developing latent friction ridge transfers (fingerprints) using powders, chemical compounds, lifting tape, and other techniques.

In this exercise you will work without a partner.

The Scenario

There has been a robbery at 9001 W. State St., Anytown, DE. The victim is the Anytown University, at the Liberal Arts Building. The room number given was 109. Another CSI team has processed the scene, and they have collected several pieces of evidence. They have requested another CSI (you) to come to the scene so that the evidence can be transferred and processed in the lab while the first CSI team continues to process a secondary scene associated with the robbery. CSI Benet will turn the evidence over to you.

The evidence has been collected and marked; however, you will inventory each piece. You will write a supplemental report, completing the top half (field information area). In the narrative, you will state "Evidence transfer from CSI Benet" and then detail how and what you did to the evidence in your attempts to recover latent fingerprints from them.

You return to the lab with the evidence and process it for latent fingerprints.
Report forms you will need to submit:

1. The case number is 0000-007-B.
2. The inventory control number is I-0000-007-B.
3. You will need to complete the following forms:
   a. Crime scene investigator's supplemental report
   b. Inventory sheet. (The latents are not inventoried, but the items from which they were recovered are inventoried.)
   c. Laboratory submission request

The laboratory work will consist of the following:

1. Process a piece of white paper using the "magna powder" method. You will protect the prints with tape, and mark and submit them for the purpose of comparison with AFIS (Automated Fingerprint Identification System).
2. You will process a white piece of paper using the ninhydrin method, protect the prints with tape, and mark and submit them for the purpose of comparison with AFIS.

3. You will dust the colored bottle for latents and lift, mark, photo image, and submit any that are recovered for the purpose of comparison with AFIS.

4. You will dust the clear bottle for latents and lift, mark, and submit any that are recovered for the purpose of comparison with AFIS.

5. You will dust the clear cup for latents using fluorescent powder.

6. You will take one good set of inked impressions (of another person, *not your own*).

Fingerprint Form

Last Name	Middle Name	First Name	Birth Date	MM DD YYYY

Sex	Race	Height	Weight	Eyes	Hair	Skin	Agency & Address

Social Security Number	SID Number	FBI Number

Address	Occupation

Place of Birth	Citizenship	Alien Number	Scars, Marks, Tattoos

Right Thumb	Right Index	Right Middle	Right Ring	Right Little

Left Thumb	Left Index	Left Middle	Left Ring	Left Little

Left Fingers	Left Thumb	Right Thumb	Right Fingers

Crime Scene Investigator's
Supplemental Report

Report Classification [   ]   Case Number [   ]

Date/Time [   ]   Type of Location [   ]   Agency [   ]   Investigator [   ]

Victim's Name [   ]   Victim's Address [   ]

Inventory Control Number [   ]   Images Taken [   ]

Evidence Collected   **Photo Images**

1		11		1		11	
2		12		2		12	
3		13		3		13	
4		14		4		14	
5		15		5		15	
6		16		6		16	
7		17		7		17	
8		18		8		18	
9		19		9		19	
10		20		10		20	

Narrative:

Signature   Supervisor's Signature

Note: Start listing photo images on this report - if additional
space is needed use photo image continuation report.   Page [   ]

Narrative Continued: **Note: Do not print or use this page unless additional space is needed.**

Signature	Supervisor's Signature	Page

Inventory Sheet

Case Number [_____]

Date/Time [_____]   Agency [_____]   Investigator [_____]

Type of Case [_____]   Inventory Control Number [_____]

Item No.	Quantity	Description of Items

Note: Item numbers above should be the same as those on the report form and the inventory form. Items recovered from separate locations or recovered under a different case number should be listed on separate lab submission sheets. Describe below pertinent information that could help in examination or testing (required).

Case Info

Submitting Officer	Date/Time	
Signature		Page

Laboratory Submission
Request

Report Classification [   ]   Case Number [   ]

Date/Time [   ]   Agency [   ]   Investigator [   ]

Victim's Name [   ]   Victim's Address [   ]

Type of Case [   ]   Inventory Control Number [   ]

Item No.	Description of Item	Type of Test or Examination Requested	Returned to Agency Date

Note: Item numbers above should be the same as those on the report form and the inventory form. Items from separate locations or recovered under a different case number should be listed on separate lab submission sheets. Describe below pertinent information that could help in examination or testing (required).

Case Info

Submitting Officer	Lab Person Receiving	Date/Time
Signature	Signature	Page

Notes

Chapter 8

Close-Up/Bench Photo Imaging

Goal: The goal of this exercise is to practice and learn close-up, "bench," or re-photo imaging for record. Many times an object collected at a crime scene cannot be photo imaged well due to scene lighting conditions, adverse topographical conditions, or weather conditions. We take images at the scene as best as we can and then bring the evidence or objects of interest into the lab. It is here that we have much better control over light, angle, and other conditions. The weather is no longer an issue. This type of photo imaging is also referred to as bench photo imaging, re-photography, and photo imaging for record. Close-up, bench, or re-photo imaging for record is not macro photo imaging. Macro photo imaging refers to photo imaging of a 1:1 ratio or closer. A special lens is required.

In this exercise you will work without a partner.

Procedure:

1. Turn off the flash on your camera and use incandescent light sources.
2. The first image will be the photo ID.
3. Photo image all the items in the container provided. Take each item with and without scale.
4. Use the appropriate background paper to take the best image. Several images may need to be taken to discover which paper works best.
5. Move the light source to add and reduce light from one side or the other.
6. Subtractive lighting can also be used to enhance your images.
7. The listing sheet should have a description of each of the photo images that you have taken.

Images should be in focus and viewable.

Name: _____ **Date:** _____

Print your photo images and turn them in with this listing sheet.

Image Description	Amb.	Flash	Special Lighting, Tool, or Technique

Image Description	Amb.	Flash	Special Lighting, Tool, or Technique

Image Description	Amb.	Flash	Special Lighting, Tool, or Technique

Notes

Goal: The goal of this exercise is to learn and practice the technique of wafting.

In this exercise you will work without a partner.

In this case, you are not a CSI. You are the lab personnel designated to work the case signed in by CSI Grissom of the Crime Scene Investigation Unit. Your case number is 0000-009. The inventory control number is I-0000-009. This is a fire case, suspected to be arson, and perhaps more. Grissom has signed in 10 pieces of evidence: A, B, C, D, E, F, G, H, I, and J (Fig. 9.1). You will examine them and make detailed notes describing your methods and your results.

Your notes and report will be written with all pertinent case information, listing each individual piece of evidence (identified by letter), the method that you used to test the item, and what you have observed and discovered. Notations should be made of color, viscosity, and, of course, odor.

Wafting

The technique of wafting is relatively simple. The sample, enclosed in an airtight container—preferably a plastic bottle, is held in the hands for several minutes. This raises the temperature slightly and allows the liquid to give off vapors. The container is then held at arm's length, and the top is removed (Fig. 9.2). Wave the hand to move the air above the bottle toward your nose. Take shallow breaths until an odor is detected. If nothing is detected at arm's length, gently inch the container closer and closer to your nose (Fig. 9.3). Caution: Do not begin by holding the container directly under your nose as the substance in the container may be volatile, such as household ammonia. Most people will be able to detect and identify most of the substances. Use the report of laboratory findings.

Accelerants

The most commonly used accelerants are petrol, kerosene, mineral turps, and diesel. These accelerants (ignitable fluids) are generally complex mixtures of hydrocarbon molecules. These hydrocarbons have similar chemical properties; however, their boiling points vary and cover a wide range of values. This variation causes the accelerants to alter their composition during the evaporation process. The more volatile hydrocarbons evaporate at a faster rate, leaving the heavier hydrocarbons in the debris, and after a period of time the accelerant becomes less volatile and less abundant.

The human sense of smell can correctly identify the presence of accelerants, even in trace amounts. This ability varies among investigators, as the sense of smell is like most other senses and can become

Figure 9.1
Here the examiner is holding a container with a suspect liquid at arm's length. He has opened the top and is waving or "waft-ing" the vapors from the container toward his nose. He is taking shallow breaths so that if the liquid is volatile or offensive, e.g., household ammonia, he can keep his exposure to a minimum. (Smelling salts, a compound used to revive unconscious persons, contains ammonia.)

highly developed through experience, or it can become impaired either temporarily or permanently. When smelling fire debris, the investigator is actually sampling the headspace above the debris and noting the chemical fingerprint of the headspace. Then, using one's discriminatory powers by comparing the finger-print with those stored in one's memory, a decision can be made as to the possible presence of an accelerant or ignitable liquid. A wine taster uses a similar technique, and the taster's highly developed sense of smell can detect extremely minute variations in the chemical fingerprint of a wine among a background of water and ethanol. The same test performed by scientific analysis and scientific interpretation requires a consider-able amount of time and expertise.

Figure 9.2
The examiner is moving the suspect liquid close until his olfactory senses detect a recognizable odor.

Laboratory Submission Request

Report Classification	Fire
Case Number	0000-009

Date/Time	00/00/00	Agency	Crime Scene Unit	Investigator	Grissom

Victim's Name	Apu	Victim's Address	lst & 2nd, Springfield, Kentucky

Type of Case	Fire	Inventory Control Number	I-0000-009

Item No.	Description of Item	Type of Test or Examination Requested	Returned to Agency Date
A	Unknown fluid	Presumptive test for Ignitable Fluid	
B	Unknown fluid	Presumptive test for Ignitable Fluid	
C	Unknown fluid	Presumptive test for Ignitable Fluid	
D	Unknown fluid	Presumptive test for Ignitable Fluid	
E	Unknown fluid	Presumptive test for Ignitable Fluid	
F	Unknown fluid	Presumptive test for Ignitable Fluid	
G	Unknown fluid	Presumptive test for Ignitable Fluid	
H	Unknown fluid	Presumptive test for Ignitable Fluid	
I	Unknown fluid	Presumptive test for Ignitable Fluid	
J	Unknown fluid	Presumptive test for Ignitable Fluid	
end			

Note: Item numbers above should be the same as those on the report form and the inventory form. Items from separate locations or recovered under a different case number should be listed on separate lab submission sheets. Describe below pertinent information that could help in examination or testing (required).

Case Info	10 bottles of unknown fluid found in the Quickey Mart by the manager, Apu, after a male subject started a fire in a trash container. Presumptive test the fluid for ignitable fluid. If positive send to Mass Spec for confirmation. END

Submitting Officer	*Grissom*	Lab Person Receiving		Date/Time	00/00/00
Signature	*Grissom*	Signature		Page	1 of 1

Report of Laboratory Findings

Lab Personnel Name:	Lab Section: Trace	Case Type:
Officer Name:	Date In:	Date Out:

Sample	Describe item in detail. Viscosity, color, etc.	Identity of item
A		
B		
C		
D		
E		
F		
G		
H		
I		
J		

Returned to Agency By:	Lab Section: Trace	Case Type:
Officer Name:	Date Returned:	Officer Initials:

Notes

Chapter 10

CSI vs. Real CSI

Goal: The goal of this exercise is to test your CSI abilities. In other words, "What is TV and what is real life?"

In this exercise you will work without a partner.

View an episode of *CSI* and observe any mistakes the cast makes while performing as CSIs. Remember that they are actors, not real crime scene investigators. Also indicate the correct method of crime scene investigation that would be used in the real world. Record your observations and comments on the form that follows.

Name: _____ **Date:** _____ **Episode Title:** _____

	CSI Mistakes	What Is the Correct Method?
1		
2		
3		
4		
5		
6		
7		
8		
9		
10		
11		
12		
13		
14		
15		
16		
17		
18		
19		
20		
21		
22		
23		
24		
25		

Notes

Chapter

Advanced Fingerprints

Goal: The goal of this exercise is to practice and learn several advanced techniques for recovering latent fingerprints.

In this exercise you will work without a partner.

The Scenario

Little Archie Bunker, 9 years old, was allegedly kidnapped from a local playground while in the custody of his babysitter. The scene was worked by Grissom and company, and four items were submitted. We will stipulate to the fact that each piece of evidence was properly collected and packaged. Note: All items will be in the bag and not packaged separately—you will accept them and treat them as if they were packaged separately.

This time you are the lab personnel assigned to recover latents using lab techniques, not a CSI. There are times that evidence is collected at a scene, but the methods required to develop latent friction ridge impressions is more than can be done in the field. These must be done in the lab. You will receive the evidence and process it as requested by the submitting CSI. Each student will receive a bag of evidence. In each bag will be:

1. A note and its envelope
2. A glass bottle
3. A shell casing
4. A plastic cup

Sign the evidence in and make your examination. Complete the report of laboratory findings which will go back to Grissom. On the sheet, state the results and the method (step by step) used to arrive at the conclusions stated, along with observations. Remember that this is a formal report that will eventually go to court. Take photo images as necessary to make and support your findings. Use the photo sheet to itemize your photographs.

Lab Protocol

1. Observe proper universal precautions. Use gloves, eye protection, and lab aprons.
2. Process patent prints in suspect blood on the bottle (Fig. 11.1).
   a. Make a visual exam of the item.
   b. Use an inherent light source to examine the evidence. A white light such as a gooseneck desk lamp works well.

Figure 11.1
This vial has a latent fingerprint in blood, barely visible.

    c. Place the object in a bath of ethanol 70% for 10 minutes. One would normally think that this would wash off the blood. It does not. Do not rub or touch the area where the print is suspected, however, during this step.

    d. Remove the object and place it in a bath of "amido black solution A" for 3 minutes. This is the dye solution. Although it is called amido black, the dye is actually a shade of dark blue.

    e. Remove the object from the dye and allow it to drip for several seconds.

    f. Place the object in "amido black solution B" for about a minute. This is the "fixer." It fixes and makes permanent the latent on the glass.

    g. Remove and allow the glass to air dry.

    h. Photo image the print. Place a white piece of paper inside the glass to use as a backing. Be sure to use a scale. The image of the latent is useless if it cannot be sized to 1:1 ratio (Fig. 11.2).

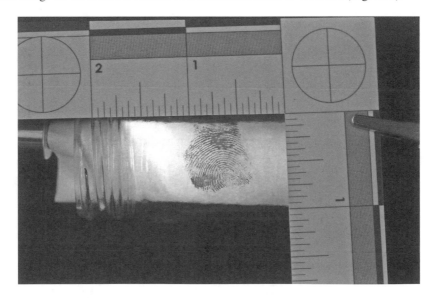

Figure 11.2
This vial has been processed using amido black solution.

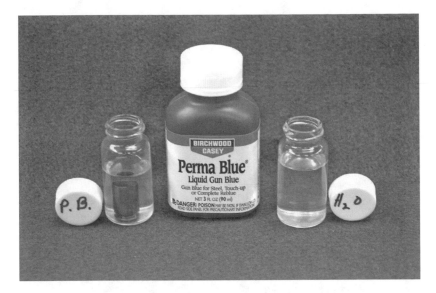

Figure 11.3
Perma Blue gun bluing available from Walmart. Two parts water to one part Perma Blue. After you see the latent developed, remove from Perma Blue and place in distilled water to stop the reaction. You may return it to the Perma Blue for more development, but remember you cannot go back. If it is too dark, it stays too dark.

3. Process shell casing.

   a. Prepare two small containers. Small Dixie cups work very well.

   b. In one, place a solution of Perma Blue® (gun bluing—available at Walmart). Other brands of bluing will also work; however, the Walmart Perma Blue has been tested for strength and duration. The compound should be one part Perma Blue to two parts distilled water.

   c. Prepare a second container with distilled water only.

   d. Use forceps to pick up the shell casing. Plastic forceps are best because they do not scratch the shell casing.

   e. Place the shell casing in the cup containing the Perma Blue (Fig. 11.3). Watch it carefully. When the print starts to show, remove the shell casing and place it in the second container to stop the reaction.

   f. Examine and photo image the print.

   g. You can put the shell casing back in the Perma Blue to make the latent darker. Use the water to stop the reaction.

   h. Note: This works best on brass shell casings. It will not work on aluminum or other metals that do not react with gun bluing.

4. Process the note and envelope.

   a. Using forceps, carefully remove the note from the envelope.

   b. Use forceps, even though you are wearing gloves. (Gloves can smear a latent, leave a glove imprint, or create an "overlay" [one print on top of another]).

   c. Spray the paper note with ninhydrin. Saturate the paper. Do this under a fume hood, outside, or in a well-ventilated area because one of the components of the ninhydrin is acetic acid.

   d. Lay a piece of brown kraft paper under and over the saturated paper.

   e. Iron it with an iron turned to its highest setting. Keep the iron moving so that it does not burn the paper.

   f. After the paper seems to be drying, examine it. Latents should appear as a light purple. If there are no prints, use the iron again to apply more heat (Fig. 11.4).

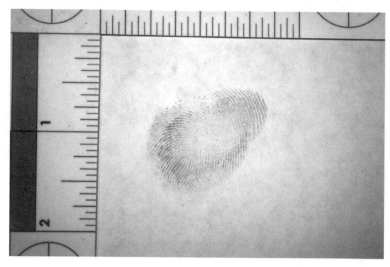

Figure 11.4
This paper was processed using ninhydrin solution and heat.

    g. Caution: Although the ninhydrin is not caustic, it will stain unprotected skin. This is because of the sebaceous oils, amino acids, and contaminates in the latent fingerprints. The ninhydrin reacts with these substances on the paper and will also react with these substances on skin. The dye does not wash off well. It wears off eventually. WEAR GLOVES.

    h. Photo image the latents. Do not forget to use a scale.

5. Cyanoacrylate fuming (Super Glue)

    a. Materials: plastic bag (gallon size), Super Glue, paper cup, foil, water, and a desk lamp with at least a 60 watt bulb, and a plastic disposable cup (with fingerprints) to fume.

    b. Fill a small paper cup ½ full water, place in bag.

    c. Squeeze a small tube of Super Glue onto an aluminum foil square.

    d. Place both in the plastic bag.

    e. Place plastic cup to fume in bag. Close bag.

    f. Turn the lamp on (with at least a 60 watt bulb) and aim at bag, 10"–12" from bulb. Make sure bulb does not come in contact with the bag.

    g. Leave bulb (heat) on for about 45 min. (Fig. 11.5).

    h. Monitor the progress of the fuming. When you see a whitish-colored latent appear, give it about 5 minutes more, then turn off the lamp.

    i. Open the bag in a well-ventilated area or under a fume hood.

    j. Remove the plastic cup and examine it under a bright light.

    k. Unlike on TV, you are still not done. You will need to use a dye or fingerprint dusting powder on the latent to make it truly visible. Fluorescent powder works well. Specific dyes such as Ardrox or Basic Yellow work better.

    l. Photograph the latent. Do not forget the scale. Submit the photo with scale for comparison by the fingerprint examiner, not the cup.

Figure 11.5
Sequence of cyanoacrylate (Super Glue) fuming.

Laboratory Submission Request
Forensic Science Laboratory

Date: 10.15.06 Time:1344 hrs.	Case #: 0000-011	Case Type: Kidnapping	Inventory #: I-000-011
Location of Incident: 4131 S Forrest Ave, Yourtown, IN		Agency Name: **Purdue CSI**	
Victim Name: **Archie Bunker**		Investigator: **Grissom**	

Item	Description of Item	Type of Test or Examination Requested	Returned to Agency: Date & Initial
1	Note with envelope	Examine for latents	
2	Small bottle with patent print in suspect blood	Recover patent print in suspect blood and evaluate for comparison	
3	Shell casing	Examine for latents, use Perma-Blue technique	
4	Plastic cup	Examine for latents—Cyanoacrylate	
	End		

Note: Item number corresponds to item number of evidence. If recovered at a different location, under a different case number (or supplementary number/letter), a separate submission should be used.

Describe any pertinent information that may aid in the examination and/or testing of this submission
Victim, Archie Bunker m/w/9 was apparently abducted from a playground near home. Victim was in the custody of babysitter (f/w/15). Bottle with patent print in suspect blood and a length of duct tape were located at the scene. A note was later delivered to the victim's home. END.

Person Submitting (Printed)		Lab Personnel Receiving (Printed)	Date:
Grissom			Time:
Person Submitting (Signature)		Lab Personnel Receiving (Signature)	

Report of Laboratory Findings

Name:	Lab Section: Fingerprints	Case Type:
Officer Name:	Date In:	Date Out:
Case Number:	Inventory Control Number:	

Item	Describe Item in Detail. Viscosity, Color, Etc.	Identity of Item
1		
2		
3		
4		

Returned to Agency By:	Lab Section: Fingerprints	Case Type:
Officer Name:	Date Returned:	Officer Initials:

Photo Images Taken of Evidence

Name:	Case Number: Inventory Control Number:
Image Description	Special Lighting, Tool, or Technique

Notes

Chapter 12

Presumptive Testing for the Presence of Blood

Goal: The goal of this exercise is to practice and learn presumptive testing for the presence of blood on various substrates.

In this exercise you will work without a partner.

Presumptive testing, or field testing, tells us only that there is blood present. It may or may not be human blood, but if the test is positive, then some type of blood is present. Once the test is completed and a positive reaction is observed, the sample should be sent to the lab to have a confirmatory test done. A presumptive test may not be used in court as proof that an item had blood on it. A confirmatory test can be used as proof of the presence of blood. A precipitin test may also be done in the lab as a confirmatory test for *human blood*.

We will be working with the Kastle-Meyer (Fig. 12.1) and the o-Tolidine (Fig. 12.2) tests. The o-Tolidine in the test is a carcinogen; however, we are in contact with many carcinogens every day such as tobacco and gasoline. Nevertheless, it is only wise to take proper laboratory precautions, which is why we say that gloves must be worn.

Safety: Wear Gloves!

Kastle-Meyer Presumptive Blood Test—Directions

1. Add two drops of alcohol to the swab. This step facilitates the transfer of the suspected blood to the cotton swab. This step can be eliminated, but for very small concentrations of blood, the use of alcohol is suggested. Note: Distilled water can also be used in this step.

2. With the alcohol on the swab, rub the cotton tip on the area that has suspected blood present. Note: The area may not appear to have blood on it. This test works on very small amounts of blood.

3. Add two drops of phenolphthalein to the swab. At this point you will not see a color change. You will, however, see the color of the phenolphthalein on the swab.

4. Add two drops of hydrogen peroxide to the swab. At this point, if there is blood present, you should see an immediate color change. Blood is indicated if a bright pink color is observed within 5 seconds or less. If the swab turns pink after 30 seconds or more, the test is inconclusive.

5. If a pink color is observed after the phenolphthalein but before the hydrogen peroxide, contaminants are present that invalidate the test. This could be the case if the substance is a red dye.

6. Use a small adhesive sticker to mark the swab. Mark it with the location recovered (bathroom sink), your initials, and the case number.

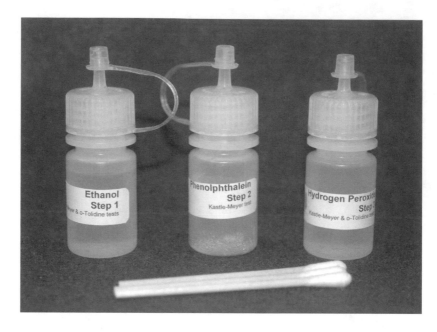

Figure 12.1
The Kastle-Meyer presumptive blood test kit. The kit contains ethyl alcohol 70%, phenolphthalein solution, and hydrogen peroxide 3%.

7. Set in a drying rack. (This can be a simple piece of Styrofoam or an expensive forensic manufactured drying rack.)

8. Perform a positive and negative control for this test. (See below.)

o-Tolidine Presumptive Blood Test—Directions

1. Add two drops of alcohol to the swab. This step facilitates the transfer of the suspected blood to the cotton swab. This step can be eliminated, but for very small concentrations of blood, the use of alcohol is suggested.

2. With the alcohol on the swab, rub the cotton tip on the area that has suspected blood present. Note: The area may not appear to have blood on it. This test works on very small amounts of blood.

3. Add two drops of o-Tolidine to the swab. At this point you will not see a color change. You will see the color of the o-Tolidine on the swab.

4. Add two drops of hydrogen peroxide to the swab. At this point, if there is blood present, you should see an immediate color change. Blood is indicated if a blue/green color is observed within 5 seconds or less. If the swab turns blue/green after 30 seconds or more, the test is inconclusive.

6. If a blue color is observed after the o-Tolidine but before the hydrogen peroxide, contaminants are present that invalidate the test.

7. Use a small adhesive sticker to mark the swab. Mark it with the location recovered (bathroom sink), your initials, and the case number.

8. Set in a drying rack. (This can be a simple piece of Styrofoam or an expensive forensic manufactured drying rack.)

9. Perform a positive and negative control for this test.

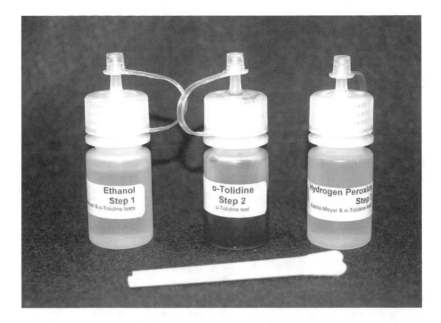

Figure 12.2
The o-Tolidine presumptive test kit. The kit contains ethyl alcohol 70%, o-Tolidine solution, and hydrogen peroxide 3%.

Positive and Negative Controls—Directions

Positive Control

After you have applied alcohol to the swab, rub it on a *known* sample of blood. This sample normally is a part of each blood testing kit. After this step, follow the same procedure used to test an unknown sample. A positive color should be obtained. If a negative result is observed after a known positive is tested, the kit is bad (contaminated) and should not be used.

Negative Control

After you have applied alcohol to the swab, immediately proceed to the next step, and then the final step. If a positive result is observed after a known *negative* is tested, the kit is bad (contaminated) and should not be used.

Packaging the Evidence—Directions

1. After the samples have been air dried in the rack, place each individual sample in a separate paper envelope or paper type container. Never use plastic. Use paper that breathes. We do not want the suspect blood (yes, until it has been through a confirmatory test, it is still referred to as "suspect blood") to decompose due to bacteria or mold. This will destroy the sample.
2. Seal it and document it as you would any other type of evidence.

Laboratory Submission Request
Forensic Science Laboratory

Date: 10.15.06 Time: 1344 hrs.	Case #: 0000-011 A	Case Type: Kidnapping	Inventory #: I-000-011 A
Location of Incident: 4131 S. Forrest Ave. Yourtown, IN		Agency Name:	
Victim Name: **Archie Bunker**		Investigator: **Grissom**	

Item	Description of Item	Type of Test or Examination Requested	Returned to Agency: Date & Initial
1	Substrate with suspect blood	Presumptive test for presence of blood	
2	Substrate with suspect blood	Presumptive test for presence of blood	
3	Substrate with suspect blood	Presumptive test for presence of blood	
4	Substrate with suspect blood	Presumptive test for presence of blood	
5	Substrate with suspect blood	Presumptive test for presence of blood	
6	Substrate with suspect blood	Presumptive test for presence of blood	
7	Substrate with suspect blood	Presumptive test for presence of blood	
8	Substrate with suspect blood	Presumptive test for presence of blood	
9	Substrate with suspect blood	Presumptive test for presence of blood	
10	Substrate with suspect blood	Presumptive test for presence of blood	
	END		

Note: Item number corresponds to item number of evidence. If recovered at a different location, under a different case number (or supplementary number/letter), a separate submission should be used.

Describe any pertinent information that may aid in the examination and/or testing of this submission.
Victim, Archie Bunker m/w/9 was apparently abducted from a playground near home. Victim was in the custody of babysitter (f/w/15). Bottle with patent print in suspect blood and a length of duct tape were located at the scene. A note was later delivered to the victim's home. Additional items (10) collected which may have blood on them END.

Person Submitting (Printed)		Lab Personnel Receiving (Printed)	Date:
Grissom			Time:
Person Submitting (Signature)		Lab Personnel Receiving (Signature)	

Report of Laboratory Findings

Name:	Lab Section:	Case Type:
Officer Name:	Date In:	Date Out:
Case Number:	Inventory Control Number:	

Item	Describe Item in Detail. Viscosity, Color, Etc.	Identity of Item
1		
2		
3		
4		
5		
6		
7		
8		
9		
10		

Returned to Agency By:	Lab Section: Trace	Case Type:
Officer Name:	Date Returned:	Officer Initials:

Photo Images Taken of Evidence

Name:	Case Number: Inventory Control Number:
Image Description	Special Lighting, Tool, or Technique

Notes

Chapter 13

Blood Patterns

Goal: The goal of this exercise is to practice and learn that blood acts consistently the same when dropped or spattered.

In this exercise you will work without a partner.

This exercise will be a lab experiment. We will look at and experiment with the properties of blood. There are three parts. Each part has an assignment.

Part A. Dropped Blood Patterns

1. Lean a piece of cardboard against a wall (Fig. 13.1)
2. Measure the angle at which the cardboard is leaning with a protractor and record the angle.
3. Dispense a drop of blood from a height of about 3 feet. Mark it as #1.
4. Photo image the drop. Do not forget to use a scale.
5. Change the angle. Measure the angle.
6. Dispense a drop of blood from a height of about 3 feet. Mark it as #2.

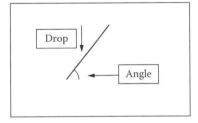

Figure 13.1
This drawing indicates the dropping of blood straight down (passive).

7. Photo image the drop. Do not forget to use a scale.
8. Change the angle. Measure the angle.
9. Dispense a drop of blood from a height of about 3 feet. Mark it as #3.
10. Photo image the drop. Do not forget to use a scale.
11. Change the angle. Measure the angle.
12. Dispense a drop of blood from a height of about 3 feet. Mark it as #4.
13. Photo image the drop. Do not forget to use a scale.
14. Change the angle. Measure the angle.
15. Dispense a drop of blood from a height of about 3 feet. Mark it as #5.
16. Photo image the drop. Do not forget to use a scale.
17. Compare your drops with the angle of impact sheet in this exercise.
18. Now under your measurement, write the angle most closely represented in the angle of impact sheet, such as 12 degrees/10 degrees. Write your name and the date on this cardboard. Use Figure 13.2 to compare your angled drops.

Figure 13.2
This figure shows impact spatters at various angles.

Part B. Identifying Blood Spatter Patterns

There are many types of spatter patterns:

1. High Velocity. Sometimes produced by a gun-shot, it is also called misting. (Approximately 100 feet/second.)

2. Medium Velocity. This can be produced by an object bearing blood being struck by a baseball bat. (Approximately 6 to 25 feet/second.)

3. Low Velocity. This can be produced from a hand bearing blood, swinging as if someone is walking. (Approximately up to 5 feet/second.)

4. Passive. This is produced from bleeding straight down with no movement. This is usually considered 90 degrees. If the drop is round and there is no side that protrudes more than any of the other sides, there is no direction (Fig. 13.3). This is a passive spatter. There are several subcategories:

   a. Drops

   b. Drips

   c. Pools

   d. Clots

Figure 13.3
This is a close-up of a 90 degree drop. It has traveled straight down and indicates no direction.

5. Void, Shadow, or "Ghosting." A void is seen when there is an object between the blood path and the terminal location such as the wall. If a lamp is between the blood and the wall, there will be a blank space (no blood) where the lamp was positioned.

6. Transfer. This occurs when blood is moved from one surface to another. There are two subcategories.

   a. Wipe. This occurs when object A (which has blood on it) comes in contact with object B (with no blood on it). Blood is transferred from A to B.

   b. Swipe. This occurs when object B has blood on it and object A does not. Object A came in contact with object B and moved the blood by swiping it.

7. Arterial Spurt or Gush. This occurs when an artery is cut. Blood spurts out with great force and in a large quantity.

8. Castoffs. This happens when blood is released or "thrown" from a blood-bearing object in motion.

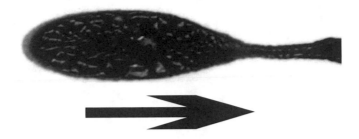

Figure 13.4
This drop has a "tail." The tail indicates the direction of the drop.

On four separate pieces of 8½" × 11" paper, create four different types of patterns. Mark each with the type of spatter you created. Write your name and the date on each paper.

Part C. Direction of Blood

Direction can be determined by observing the drop. If one side protrudes more than the other sides, then there is a direction. The direction is determined from the small point on one end of the elongated drop. For example, the direction of the drop in Figure 13.4 is moving from left to right.

Use an object to create castoffs. Create at least three 8½" × 11" sheets each with a castoff. Indicate the direction for each. Write your name and the date on each paper.

Blood Angle of Impact

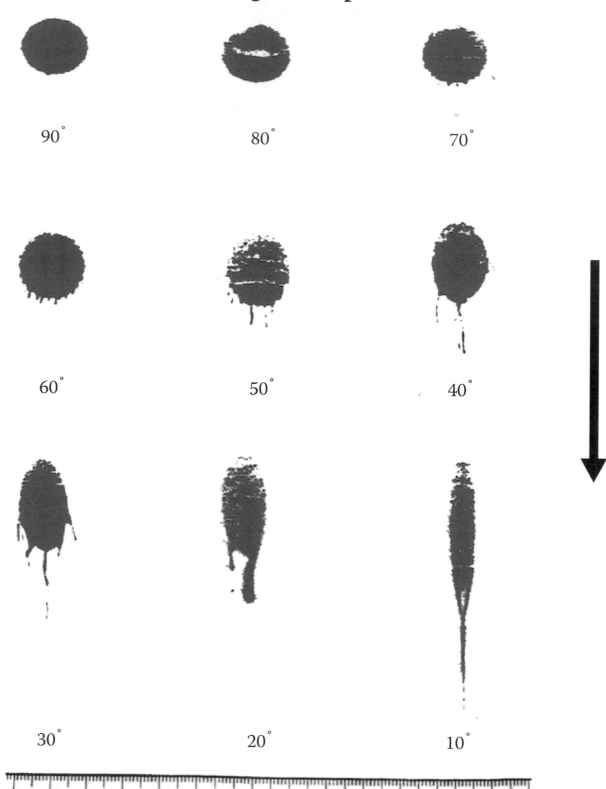

Notes

Chapter 14

Car Crash, or Is It?

Goal: The goal of this exercise is to process the scene of a car crash, to be meticulous in your investigation, and to always enter a case with an open mind with no preconceived notions.

Remember: "If it walks like a duck, quacks like a duck, looks like a duck, it may be a goose wearing a duck costume."

In this exercise you will work as a team. The labor may be divided. This is both good and bad. You rely not only on your own expertise, but you also have to rely on that of your partners. They must do their part and meet with the rest of the team to exchange information, images, and drawings.

One team member may take the images; one team member may collect, bag, and tag the evidence; and one team member may take measurements and draw the scene diagram. Only one team member will actually physically turn in evidence, but all team members will list it on their reports. Only one team member will actually take the photo images, but he or she will share with the other team members so that each team member turns in a set of images and lists them on their reports. Only one team member will draw the scene drawing, but he or she will share the drawing with the other members so that each team member can turn in a copy of the drawing.

The Scenario

It is a very busy morning for your CSI unit. Another CSI team has been sent to 469 Maple St., Yourtown, OH, in reference to a found body (possible homicide). Your team apparently lucked out and got the car crash. Maybe.

1. Investigate a fatal auto crash located at Rt. 26 and Klondike, Yourtown, Ohio. Cross intersection State Route 998.
2. The case number is 0000-014.
3. The inventory control number is I-0000-014.
4. Take the number of photos necessary to document and record the scene.
5. The photos will be listed in order on the CSI investigator's report. (If there are *more* photos than will fit on the original case report, use a photo image continuation report to continue, but start on the investigator's report.)
6. Collect evidence as necessary.
7. Take measurements and create a scene drawing.
8. Fingerprints? Possibly to prove who was driving. Remember we dust on the inside driver's side for latents to help establish the identity of the driver.
9. Concerning evidence, your instructor will have detailed information concerning its collection.

You will need the following:

    a. Crime scene investigator's report

    b. Vehicle processing report (Remember: If there is a narrative on the investigator's case report, draw a single line through the narrative section on the vehicle processing report. You only need one narrative.)

    c. Graph paper, ¼" × ¼". In pencil draw a diagram of scene.

    d. Photo image continuation report (if necessary)

    e. Evidence continuation report (if necessary)

    f. Laboratory submission request

    g. Body diagram report

    h. Evidence

    i. Photo images

Crime Scene
Investigator's Report

Report Classification		Case Number	

Date/Time		Type of Location		Agency		Investigator	

Victim's Name		Victim's Address	

Injuries		Taken for Treatment		Victim Rape Kit		Suspect in Custody	

Suspect Rape Kit		Weapon		Gunshot Residue		Gun Sheet	

Weather		Inside Temperature		Outside Temperature		Crime Scene Drawing	

Alcohol		Drugs		Lighting Conditions	

Vehicle		Make		Model		Year		Color	

Vehicle Sheet		License Plate		License Plate State	

Other Distinguishing Characteristics	

Inventory Control Number		Images Taken	

Evidence Collected				**Photo Images**			
1		23		1		23	
2		24		2		24	
3		25		3		25	
4		26		4		26	
5		27		5		27	
6		28		6		28	
7		29		7		29	
8		30		8		30	
9		31		9		31	
10		32		10		32	
11		33		11		33	
12		34		12		34	
13		35		13		35	
14		36		14		36	
15		37		15		37	
16		38		16		38	
17		39		17		39	
18		40		18		40	
19		41		19		41	
20		42		20		42	
21		43		21		43	
22		44		22		44	

Note: Start listing photo images on this report - if additional space is needed use photo image continuation report.

Signature		Page	

Narrative:

| Signature | Supervisor's Signature | Page |

Inventory Sheet

Case Number [   ]

Date/Time [   ]   Agency [   ]   Investigator [   ]

Type of Case [   ]   Inventory Control Number [   ]

Item No.	Quantity	Description of Items

Note: Item numbers above should be the same as those on the report form. Items recovered from separate locations or recovered under a different case number should be listed on separate lab submission sheets.
Describe below pertinent information that could help in examination or testing (required).

Case Info

Submitting Officer   Date/Time

Signature   Page

Vehicle Processing
Report

Report Classification [   ]   Case Number [   ]

Date/Time [   ]   Type of Location [   ]   Agency [   ]   Investigator [   ]

Victim's Name [   ]   Victim's Address [   ]

Inventory Control Number [   ]   Images Taken [   ]

Make [   ]

Model [   ]

Year [   ]

Color [   ]

Plate Number/State [   ]

VIN [   ]

Odometer [   ]

Clock/Time [   ]

Passenger Side   Top   Driver Side

Windows [   ]   Draw lines and clearly identify artifacts on the vehicle. Number them and describe in narrative.

Climate Control [   ]   Blower/Fan [   ]   Keys in Ignition [   ]   Motor Running [   ]

Radio [   ]   Exterior Temp [   ]   Interior Temp [   ]   Windows [   ]

Vehicle Length [   ]   Front Bumper to Windshield [   ]   Front Window to Rear Window [   ]

Vehicle Width [   ]   Rear Window to Rear Bumper [   ]   Lights [   ]

Other Markings [   ]

Evidence Collected				**Photo Images**			
1		11		1		11	
2		12		2		12	
3		13		3		13	
4		14		4		14	
5		15		5		15	
6		16		6		16	
7		17		7		17	
8		18		8		18	
9		19		9		19	
10		20		10		20	

Signature   Supervisor's Signature

Note: Start listing photo images on this report - if additional space is needed use photo image continuation report.   Page [   ]

Narrative Continued: Note: Do not print or use this page unless additional space is needed.

| Signature | Supervisor's Signature | Page |

Body Diagram
Report

Case Classification [   ]   Case Number [   ]

Date/Time [   ]   Type of Location [   ]   Agency [   ]   Investigator [   ]

Victim's Name [   ]   Victim's Address [   ]

Weapon [   ]   Gunshot Residue [   ]   Gun Sheet [   ]   Rape Kit [   ]   Suspect in Custody [   ]

Alcohol [   ]   Drugs [   ]   Lighting Conditions [   ]

Inventory Control Number [   ]   Images Taken [   ]

Evidence Collected				**Photo Images**			
1		23		1		23	
2		24		2		24	
3		25		3		25	
4		26		4		26	
5		27		5		27	
6		28		6		28	
7		29		7		29	
8		30		8		30	
9		31		9		31	
10		32		10		32	
11		33		11		33	
12		34		12		34	
13		35		13		35	
14		36		14		36	
15		37		15		37	
16		38		16		38	
17		39		17		39	
18		40		18		40	
19		41		19		41	
20		42		20		42	
21		43		21		43	
22		44		22		44	

Narrative:

[   ]

Note: Start listing photo images on this report - if additional space is needed use photo image continuation report.

Signature   Supervisor's Signature   Page [   ]

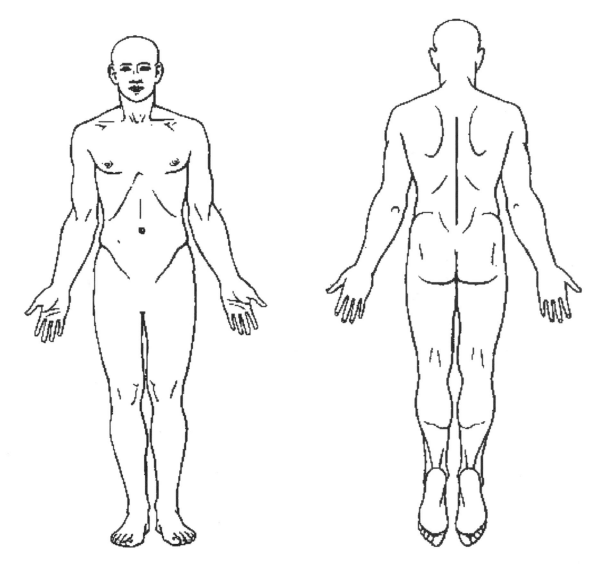

Identify artifacts.

Signature   Supervisor's Signature   Page

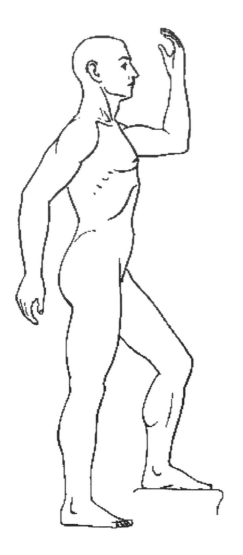 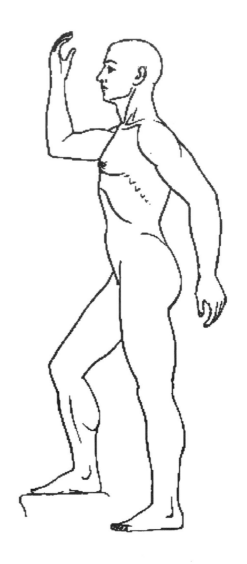

Identify artifacts:

Signature	Supervisor's Signature	Page

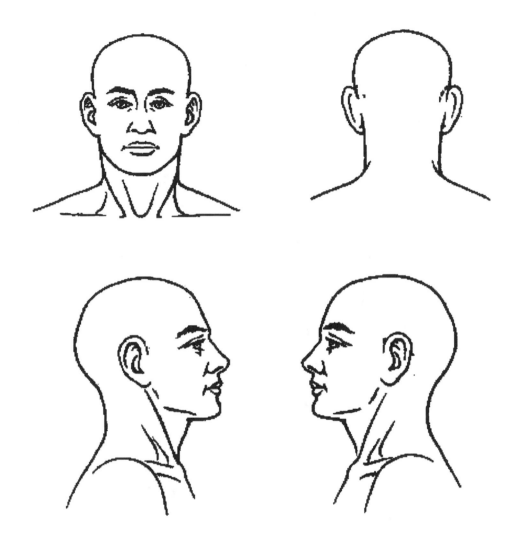

Identify artifacts.

Signature	Supervisor's Signature	Page	

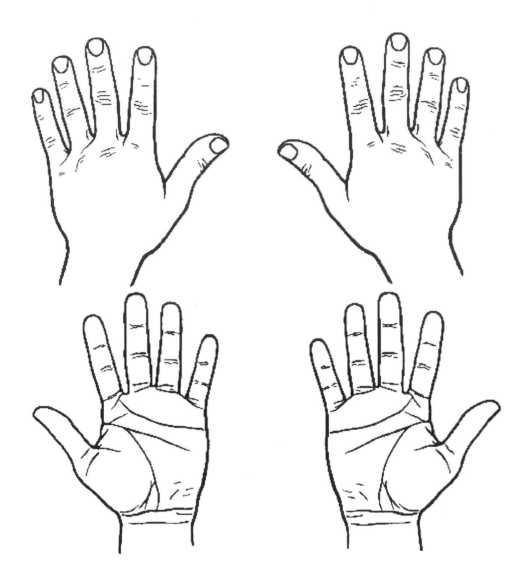

Identify artifacts

Signature	Supervisor's Signature	Page

Laboratory Submission Request

Report Classification		Case Number
Date/Time	Agency	Investigator
Victim's Name	Victim's Address	
Type of Case	Inventory Control Number	

Item No.	Description of Item	Type of Test or Examination Requested	Returned to Agency Date

Note: Item numbers above should be the same as those on the report form and the inventory form. Items from separate locations or recovered under a different case number should be listed on separate lab submission sheets. Describe below pertinent information that could help in examination or testing (required).

Case Info		
Submitting Officer	Lab Person Receiving	Date/Time
Signature	Signature	Page

Notes

Chapter 15

Toolmarks

Goal: The goal of this exercise is learn and practice the taking of toolmark impressions.

In this exercise you will work without a partner.

The Scenario

There has been a burglary at 1640 Clyde Dr., Yourtown, FL. The victim is Ned Flanders. Officer Wiggums, the uniformed officer taking the report, has discovered the POE (point of entry) as being the rear (south) kitchen door. The door is 36" wide and 7' high. The wooden edge of the door appears to have some type of mark on it. Officer Wiggums believes that the mark may be from a "jimmie" type tool and that the mark may be a toolmark.

Two tactical detectives stopped a Homer Simpson about a block away from the Flanders' home. Simpson was taken into custody after he was found to have 6,280 outstanding parking tickets. He was placed under arrest and when searched, he was found to have a screwdriver in his possession. The tactical detectives learned that you were processing a burglary scene nearby so they turned the screwdriver over to you.

General information concerning the scene:

1. Ambient temperature inside 72°F.
2. Weather outside is damp, foggy, and cool, 58°F.
3. Victim's name is Ned Flanders. He wife is deceased. They have two children, both boys, ages 9 and 10.

Report forms and items you will need to submit:

1. Crime scene investigator's report. Case number: 0000-015. Classification—burglary.
2. Inventory sheet. Inventory number: I-0000-015
3. Photo images
4. Drawing of the POE only
5. Evidence (the screwdriver and the toolmark impression)

Instructions:

1. Process the scene, specifically the POE, for toolmarks.
2. Photo image the toolmark impression on the door using oblique light. (Light source at 45 degrees to the toolmark impression.)

3. Use silicon rubber to make a casting of the toolmark at the POE. Photograph the casting using oblique light. Note: When photographing the casting, photograph with scale only.

4. Photo image the screwdriver.

5. Make a casting of the screwdriver for comparison.

6. Photo image both impressions—side by side (with scale)—and print this image full page.

Evidence:

Bag and tag the silicone rubber castings separately as evidence.

Crime Scene
Investigator's Report

Report Classification [ ] Case Number [ ]

Date/Time [ ] Type of Location [ ] Agency [ ] Investigator [ ]

Victim's Name [ ] Victim's Address [ ]

Injuries [ ] Taken for Treatment [ ] Victim Rape Kit [ ] Suspect in Custody [ ]

Suspect Rape Kit [ ] Weapon [ ] Gunshot Residue [ ] Gun Sheet [ ]

Weather [ ] Inside Temperature [ ] Outside Temperature [ ] Crime Scene Drawing [ ]

Alcohol [ ] Drugs [ ] Lighting Conditions [ ]

Vehicle [ ] Make [ ] Model [ ] Year [ ] Color [ ]

Vehicle Sheet [ ] License Plate [ ] License Plate State [ ]

Other Distinguishing Characteristics [ ]

Inventory Control Number [ ] Images Taken [ ]

Evidence Collected   **Photo Images**

#		#		#		#	
1		23		1		23	
2		24		2		24	
3		25		3		25	
4		26		4		26	
5		27		5		27	
6		28		6		28	
7		29		7		29	
8		30		8		30	
9		31		9		31	
10		32		10		32	
11		33		11		33	
12		34		12		34	
13		35		13		35	
14		36		14		36	
15		37		15		37	
16		38		16		38	
17		39		17		39	
18		40		18		40	
19		41		19		41	
20		42		20		42	
21		43		21		43	
22		44		22		44	

Note: Start listing photo images on this report - if additional space is needed use photo image continuation report.

Signature [ ] Page [ ]

Narrative:

| Signature | Supervisor's Signature | Page |

Inventory Sheet

Case Number [ ]

Date/Time [ ]   Agency [ ]   Investigator [ ]

Type of Case [ ]   Inventory Control Number [ ]

Item No.	Quantity	Description of Items

Note: Item numbers above should be the same as those on the report form. Items recovered from separate locations or recovered under a different case number should be listed on separate lab submission sheets.
Describe below pertinent information that could help in examination or testing (required).

Case Info

Submitting Officer   Date/Time

Signature   Page

Laboratory Submission
Request

Report Classification [   ]   Case Number [   ]

Date/Time [   ]   Agency [   ]   Investigator [   ]

Victim's Name [   ]   Victim's Address [   ]

Type of Case [   ]   Inventory Control Number [   ]

Item No.	Description of Item	Type of Test or Examination Requested	Returned to Agency Date

Note: Item numbers above should be the same as those on the report form and the inventory form. Items from separate locations or recovered under a different case number should be listed on separate lab submission sheets. Describe below pertinent information that could help in examination or testing (required).

Case Info

Submitting Officer	Lab Person Receiving	Date/Time
Signature	Signature	Page

Notes

Chapter **16**

Recovering a Firearm

Goal: The goal of this exercise is to learn and practice the correct method to recover a firearm.

In this exercise you will work without a partner.

The Scenario

There has been a shooting on the street at the corner of Grant and State Streets, Yourtown, IL. A man has been shot and killed. He has been tentatively identified as George Global. Grissom and Beaker have been assigned to cover the primary scene. The suspect was chased by a beat officer into a public men's restroom in the building at 901 W. State St., Yourtown, IL. The suspect, I. M. Guilty, was arrested and taken into custody in the lobby of the building. Guilty was found not to have a gun on his person when he was arrested and searched. An examination was made of the restroom by Officer Smith, who observed what appeared to be a handgun in one of the toilet bowls. He did not touch the handgun, but informed dispatch and requested a CSI team to recover the weapon. Since this is a restroom in a public building, a warrant to search the restroom is not needed.

Report forms and items you will need:

1. Crime scene entry log
2. Crime scene investigator's supplemental report. Case number: 0000-016-A. Classification—shooting.
3. Inventory sheet. Inventory control number: I-0000-016-A
4. Handgun report
5. Drawing of the restroom
6. Laboratory submission request

Instructions:

1. Process the scene, concentrating on the toilet bowl area.
2. Take measurements for your drawing.
3. Photo images should be taken to completely document the scene. Photo image the cylinder and placement of the live, spent and empty chambers.
4. In your narrative, in addition to including who, what, where, how, and why, state in detail how you made the weapon "safe," at what point you made it safe during your examination of the crime scene, and how the weapon was collected and packaged. (Making a firearm "safe" entails unloading the cartridges from the weapon, then doublechecking to be sure it will not fire.)
5. All evidence will be collected.

Crime Scene Investigator's
Supplemental Report

Report Classification [   ]   Case Number [   ]

Date/Time [   ]   Type of Location [   ]   Agency [   ]   Investigator [   ]

Victim's Name [   ]   Victim's Address [   ]

Inventory Control Number [   ]   Images Taken [   ]

Evidence Collected **Photo Images**

1		11		1		11	
2		12		2		12	
3		13		3		13	
4		14		4		14	
5		15		5		15	
6		16		6		16	
7		17		7		17	
8		18		8		18	
9		19		9		19	
10		20		10		20	

Narrative:

Signature   Supervisor's Signature

Note: Start listing photo images on this report - if additional space is needed use photo image continuation report.   Page [   ]

Narrative Continued: Note: **Do not print or use this page unless additional space is needed.**

Signature	Supervisor's Signature	Page

Inventory Sheet

Case Number [   ]

Date/Time [   ]   Agency [   ]   Investigator [   ]

Type of Case [   ]   Inventory Control Number [   ]

Item No.	Quantity	Description of Items

Note: Item numbers above should be the same as those on the report form and the inventory form. Items recovered from separate locations or recovered under a different case number should be listed on separate lab submission sheets. Describe below pertinent information that could help in examination or testing (required).

Case Info

Submitting Officer	Date/Time
Signature	Page

Photo Image
Continuation Report

Report Classification [   ] Case Number [   ]

Date/Time [   ] Type of Location [   ] Agency [   ] Investigator [   ]

Victim's Name [   ] Victim's Address [   ]

Image Number	Description of Image

Signature   Supervisor's Signature   Page [   ]

Handgun Report

Report Classification [＿＿＿＿＿＿＿＿＿＿＿] Case Number [＿＿＿＿＿＿]

Date/Time [＿＿＿＿] Type of Location [＿＿＿＿] Agency [＿＿＿＿] Investigator [＿＿＿]

Victim's Name [＿＿＿＿＿＿] Victim's Address [＿＿＿＿＿＿＿＿＿]

Revolver

Make [＿＿＿] Model [＿＿＿] Finish [＿＿＿] Serial Number [＿＿＿]

Caliber [＿＿＿] Sights [＿＿＿] Chambers [＿＿＿] Cocked [＿＿＿] Rotation [＿＿＿]

Ammunition Manufacturer [＿＿＿] Photographed [＿＿] Other Marks [＿＿＿＿]

L=Live, S=Spent, E=Empty   **Label and/or Draw Chambers**

Draw in Custom

Semi-Automatic

Make [＿＿＿] Model [＿＿＿] Finish [＿＿＿] Serial Number [＿＿＿]

Caliber [＿＿＿] Sights [＿＿＿] Chambers [＿＿＿] Cocked [＿＿＿] Photographed [＿＿]

Safety [＿＿] Round in Chamber [＿＿] Rounds in Magazine [＿＿] Magazine Capacity [＿＿]

Magazine in Weapon [＿＿] Photographed [＿＿] Other Marks [＿＿＿＿]

Ammunition Manufacturer [＿＿＿] Other Marks [＿＿＿＿]

Narrative

Image Field

Signature [＿＿＿＿＿] Supervisor's Signature [＿＿＿＿＿]

Draw single line through section not used.   Page [＿＿＿]

Narrative Continued: Note: Do not print or use this page unless additional space is needed.

Signature

Supervisor's Signature

Page

Laboratory Submission
Request

Report Classification [   ]   Case Number [   ]

Date/Time [   ] Agency [   ]   Investigator [   ]

Victim's Name [   ]   Victim's Address [   ]

Type of Case [   ]   Inventory Control Number [   ]

Item No.	Description of Item	Type of Test or Examination Requested	Returned to Agency Date

Note: Item numbers above should be the same as those on the report form and the inventory form. Items from separate locations or recovered under a different case number should be listed on separate lab submission sheets. Describe below pertinent information that could help in examination or testing (required).

Case Info

Submitting Officer	Lab Person Receiving	Date/Time
Signature	Signature	Page

Notes

Chapter 17

Interactive Virtual Crime Scene

Goal: The goal of this exercise is to learn and practice to think, not just "make the donuts" or "go through the motions." This exercise will consist of class interaction, processing the scene virtually, but with the input of the entire class and the instructor.

In this exercise you will work as a team.

The Scenario

1. As a CSI you have been dispatched to a death investigation, an apparent suicide, located at the Notel Motel, room 105, on State Route 24, Yourtown, CO, at 1545 hours. (Oh well, just what you need, overtime again.)

2. You arrive at the motel at 1615 hours.

3. The first officer on scene, Patrolman Smith, advises that the maid discovered the body of a white male subject in room 105 when she entered to clean at 1520 hours. She did not touch anything. She backed out of the room, locked it, and called 911. No one has been in the room other than the maid and Smith who checked for signs of life but found none. He called for CSIs, an investigator, and the coroner's office. He then secured the scene (the motel room). Investigator Columbo was assigned as the investigator. A wallet was found on the bed with a driver's license identifying the deceased as John T. Body. There was $87 in cash, credit cards, and a photo of a woman, torn in two.

4. Your instructor will give you a scene diagram.

5. One person on the team will document the discussion. "Case notes" will be handed in at the end of the exercise.

6. What do you do? Remember sequencing.

Module 1

You will separate into your assigned teams for 10 minutes. Decide on what is to be done, the sequence in which the steps should be performed, and note additional items of information you wish. After the 10 minutes, return to the group. Present your conclusions to the group and instructor. Conclusions and discussion should last about 15 minutes.

Module 2

After this group discussion, your instructor will give you Module 2, which contains additional information. Return to your team and discuss what the additional information means. Decide if you must change your processing sequence and what additional steps should be taken.

You will discuss the scenario utilizing the additional information for 10 minutes. Return to the group and again share your conclusions with the group and the instructor. Conclusions and discussion should last about 15 minutes.

Module 3

The autopsy was performed the morning following the incident. The preliminary autopsy report will be given to you by the instructor. Return to your team and discuss what the additional information means, and decide if you must change your processing sequence. If you must return to the scene, what additional steps should be taken, and what evidence should be submitted for analysis at the crime lab? Return to the group and again share your conclusions with the group and the instructor. Will you need a search warrant? Conclusions and discussion should last about 15 minutes.

Module 4

You will be given Module 4, which contains still more information. You will discuss the scenario for 10 minutes. At the end of this period of time, consolidate your notes and be prepared to present your findings to the group and instructor.

Teams

After the group is separated into teams of three or four students, the teams should be given 5 minutes to decide who is in charge and who will do the note taking.

Some suggested questions for the team discussion:

- How will you process the scene?
- What will you photograph?
- What specific things will you do?
- What items will you collect?
- What items will you submit?
- What information do you want from items submitted?
- Each team may ask the instructors questions.

Case Notes

Case Notes

Chapter 18

Soil

Goal: The goal of this exercise is to learn and practice looking at soil and its properties.

In this exercise you will work without a partner.

The Scenario

You are working in the lab again and will do soil analysis and comparisons. A vehicle struck a pedestrian, Archibald Zingus, on a rural stretch of US Highway 66, Yourtown, WY. The accident occurred on a dirt road. Soil samples were taken at four areas in and around the road at the crash site. The case number is 0000-018 and your inventory control number is I-0000-018 for the crash site and where the victim was found. CSI Jenkins worked the scene and has signed the evidence into the lab.

CSI Jenkins also processed the suspect's auto. The suspect's auto was found at a diner on US Route 66 at 1200 East. The vehicle was a red 1999 Toyota. This case number is 0000-018-A, and the inventory control number is I-0000-018-A for the soil evidence recovered from the suspect's auto.

Compare the samples recovered from the suspect's auto with the four samples taken from the site of the auto crash. Make detailed lab notes concerning your match or no match. Indicate what tests you performed to reach your conclusions.

Obtain the samples marked inventory control number I-0000-018, items 1, 2, 3, and 4. Obtain the sample marked inventory control number I-0000-018-A. Item 1: Weigh each and record the weights in Table 18.1. Make sure you subtract the tare weight of the container or if your scale has a tare function, be sure to use it. Weigh each sample and record the *net* weight of the soil in the lab notes, Table 18.1.

1. Compare colors of each of the items and record them in Table 18.2.
2. Using the Munsell Soil Color Chart, record the corresponding hue/value/chroma for each item in Table 18.2.
3. Place a small amount of neutral, deionized, or distilled water into each specimen in spot plate. Mix thoroughly with a stir stick. Expose a piece of pH paper in the wet soil. Determine the pH of each item and record results in Table 18.3.
4. Use the samples marked inventory control number I-0000-018, items 1, 2, 3, and 4 and the sample marked inventory control number I-0000-018-A. Item 1: Examine each sample under a stereo microscope. Make detailed observations and record them in Table 18.4. These observations should include:
   a. Color
   b. Particle size range
   c. Types and relative amount of constituents (minerals, plants, bone, shell, industrial material, other)
   d. Other unique parameters
   e. Any living materials

Lab Notes

TABLE 18.1
Soil Data Weight Sheet

Item # and Inventory Control	Collected From	Net Weight
Item 1 - I-0000-018	Road	
Item 2 - I-0000-018	Road	
Item 3 - I-0000-018	Road	
Item 4 - I-0000-018	Road	
Item 1 - I-0000-018-A	Suspect's Auto	

TABLE 18.2
Soil Color Comparison

Item # and Inventory Control	Collected From	Soil Color—Describe	Munsell Chart: Hue/ Value/Chroma
Item 1 - I-0000-018	Road		
Item 2 - I-0000-018	Road		
Item 3 - I-0000-018	Road		
Item 4 - I-0000-018	Road		
Item 1 - I-0000-018-A	Suspect's Auto		

TABLE 18.3
Soil pH Comparison Table

Item # and Inventory Control	Collected From	Soil's pH
Item 1 - I-0000-018	Road	
Item 2 - I-0000-018	Road	
Item 3 - I-0000-018	Road	
Item 4 - I-0000-018	Road	
Item 1 - I-0000-018-A	Suspect's Auto	

Based on the information recorded in Tables 18.1, 18.2, 18.3, and 18.4, determine whether the sample marked inventory control number I-0000-018-A has a common origin with any of the samples marked inventory control number I-0000-018, items 1, 2, 3, and 4. Justify your conclusions based on the data you collected. Include similar and dissimilar features of the questioned and known specimens based on your examination. Turn in your report of laboratory findings along with your lab notes (Tables 18.1, 18.2, 18.3, and 18.4) and any other notes used in your observations and conclusions.

TABLE 18.4 Soil Observation Notes From Microscopic Examination	
Item # and Inventory Control	Observations
Item 1 - I-0000-018	
Item 2 - I-0000-018	
Item 3 - I-0000-018	
Item 4 - I-0000-018	
Item 1 - I-0000-018	

Laboratory Submission Request
Forensic Science Laboratory

Date: 10.15.0000 Time: 1344 hrs.	Case #: 0000-018	Case Type: Car Crash	Inventory #: I-0000-018
Location of Incident: **US Route 66 at 500 West, Yourtown, WY**		Agency Name: **Wyoming State Police**	
Victim Name: **Archibald Zingus**		Investigator: **Jenkins**	

Item	Description of Item	Type of Test or Examination Requested	Returned to Agency: Date & Initial
1	Soil Sample – Edge of Road, North	Compare with Inventory I-0000-118-A, Item 1	
2	Soil Sample – Edge of Road, South	Compare with Inventory I-0000-118-A, Item 1	
3	Soil Sample – Center of East Bound	Compare with Inventory I-0000-118-A, Item 1	
4	Soil Sample – Center of West Bound	Compare with Inventory I-0000-118-A, Item 1	
	End		

Note: Item number corresponds to item number of evidence. If recovered at a different location, under a different case number (or supplementary number/letter), a separate submission should be used.

Describe any pertinent information that may aid in the examination and/or testing of this submission.
The victim, Archibald Zingus, was struck by a vehicle on US Route 66 at 500 West. Soil samples were taken from the site of the crash. A soil sample was taken from the suspect's auto. Route 66 at 1200 East. The vehicle was a red 1999 Toyota. End

Person Submitting (Printed)		Lab Personnel Receiving (Printed)	Date:
Jenkins			Time:
Person Submitting (Signature)		Lab Personnel Receiving (Signature)	

Laboratory Submission Request
Forensic Science Laboratory

Date: 10.15.0000 Time: 1344 hrs.	Case #: 0000-018-A	Case Type: Car Crash	Inventory #: I-0000-018-A
Location of Incident: **US Route 66 at 500 West, Yourtown, WY**		Agency Name: **Wyoming State Police**	
Victim Name: **Archibald Zingus**		Investigator: **Jenkins**	

Item	Description of Item	Type of Test or Examination Requested	Returned to Agency: Date & Initial
1	Soil Sample—Suspect's Auto	Compare with Inventory I-0000-118, Items 1, 2, 3, and 4	
End			

Note: Item number corresponds to item number of evidence. If recovered at a different location, under a different case number (or supplementary number/letter), a separate submission should be used.

Describe any pertinent information that may aid in the examination and/or testing of this submission.
The victim, Archibald Zingus, was struck by a vehicle on US Route 66 at 500 West. Soil samples were taken from the site of the crash. A soil sample was taken from the suspect's auto. Route 66 at 1200 East. The vehicle was a red 1999 Toyota. End

Person Submitting (Printed)	Jenkins	Lab Personnel Receiving (Printed)	Date:
			Time:
Person Submitting (Signature)	Jenkins	Lab Personnel Receiving (Signature)	

Report of Laboratory Findings

Name:	Lab Section: Trace	Case Type:
Officer Name:	Date In:	Date Out:
Case Number:	Inventory Control Number:	

Item	Describe Item in Detail. Viscosity, Color, Etc.	Identity of Item or Match
Item 1 I-0000-018 From Crash Site		
Item 2 I-0000-018 From Crash Site		
Item 3 I-0000-018 From Crash Site		
Item 4 I-0000-018 From Crash Site		
Item 1 I-0000-018-A From Suspect's Vehicle		

Returned to Agency By:	Lab Section: Trace	Case Type:
Officer Name:	Date Returned:	Officer Initials:

Notes

19

Forensic Entomology

Goal: The goal of this exercise is to learn and practice the collection of entomological evidence at a crime scene.

In this exercise you will work without a partner.

Forensic entomology is the study of insects associated with criminal investigations and legal matters. An important aspect of forensic entomology is assessing the succession and development of insect activity attracted to a corpse. This information is used to determine the postmortem interval (PMI), or time since death. Insect evidence associated with decomposing human remains has shown to be a very accurate means of estimating the PMI.

Insects frequently found associated with decomposing human remains include various blow flies and beetles, along with a few other insect groups. Blow flies are most often used as the primary insects in assessing the PMI.

As with other evidence collected at the crime scene, proper collection and preservation of insect evidence is of utmost importance. Along with pertinent observations, photography of the scene, and obtaining and recording temperature data, insect evidence should be given to a knowledgeable forensic entomologist (FE) for examination and assessment.

As CSIs, it is our job to properly collect and document the insect evidence at the death scene and to provide this evidence to the FE if he or she cannot be at the scene.

The Scenario

The partially decomposed, maggot-infested body of a "man" (dead pig) was discovered on June 1, 0000, in a wooded area off Route 66 and 500 West, Yourtown, OK. Other insects (adult flies, beetles, ants, etc.) may be present as well.

Process the crime scene, paying particular attention to the entomological evidence. Collect the evidence keeping in mind that this evidence will be examined by a forensic entomologist. Document the scene and your collection procedures with as much detail as possible. Take detailed photo images to back up the evidence collected.

Assignment

1. Fill out the crime scene investigator's forensic entomology collection form.

   In the narrative section of the form, include the following:

   a. Provide details of the stage of decomposition of the body and describe the surrounding environment.

    b. Provide details of what you collected and how you collected and processed the samples collected.

    c. Explain the collection procedures you used and why they were important to follow.

    d. Provide written observations on the development of live maggots collected, when they pupated, and when any adult flies emerged from your "maggot motel."

2. Collect a minimum of two vials of maggots, from two different parts of the body, properly preserved and labeled.

3. Collect at least one adult fly and another insect properly preserved and labeled in vials.

4. Provide the photo images taken at the scene and include the filled out photo listing sheet.

5. Write a letter of request to a forensic entomologist for examination and estimating the postmortem interval.

Equipment Needed for Collection

- KAA—for killing fly larvae
- Ethanol 70%—for preserving adult insects and maggots
- 4 scintillation jars/vials, approximately 0.5 ounce each
- Insect net
- No. 2 pencil
- "Maggot Motel" (see Appendix H)

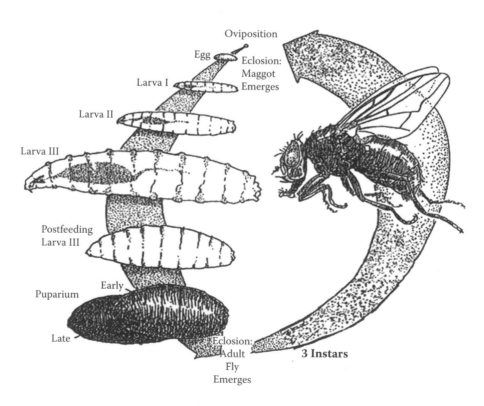

Figure 19.1
The blow fly life cycle.

Crime Scene
Investigator's Report

Report Classification [   ] Case Number [   ]

Date/Time [   ] Type of Location [   ] Agency [   ] Investigator [   ]

Victim's Name [   ] Victim's Address [   ]

Injuries [   ] Taken for Treatment [   ] Victim Rape Kit [   ] Suspect in Custody [   ]

Suspect Rape Kit [   ] Weapon [   ] Gunshot Residue [   ] Gun Sheet [   ]

Weather [   ] Inside Temperature [   ] Outside Temperature [   ] Crime Scene Drawing [   ]

Alcohol [   ] Drugs [   ] Lighting Conditions [   ]

Vehicle [   ] Make [   ] Model [   ] Year [   ] Color [   ]

Vehicle Sheet [   ] License Plate [   ] License Plate State [   ]

Other Distinguishing Characteristics [   ]

Inventory Control Number [   ] Images Taken [   ]

Evidence Collected **Photo Images**

#		#		#		#	
1		23		1		23	
2		24		2		24	
3		25		3		25	
4		26		4		26	
5		27		5		27	
6		28		6		28	
7		29		7		29	
8		30		8		30	
9		31		9		31	
10		32		10		32	
11		33		11		33	
12		34		12		34	
13		35		13		35	
14		36		14		36	
15		37		15		37	
16		38		16		38	
17		39		17		39	
18		40		18		40	
19		41		19		41	
20		42		20		42	
21		43		21		43	
22		44		22		44	

Note: Start listing photo images on this report - if additional space is needed use photo image continuation report.

Signature [   ] Page [   ]

Narrative:

_____

| Signature | Supervisor's Signature | Page |

Inventory Sheet

Case Number [   ]

Date/Time [   ]   Agency [   ]   Investigator [   ]

Type of Case [   ]   Inventory Control Number [   ]

Item No.	Quantity	Description of Items

Note: Item numbers above should be the same as those on the report form. Items recovered from separate locations or recovered under a different case number should be listed on separate lab submission sheets.
Describe below pertinent information that could help in examination or testing (required).

Case Info

Submitting Officer   Date/Time

Signature   Page

Crime Scene Investigator's Forensic Entomology Collection Form

Date: [   ]   Case Type: [   ]   Agency: [   ]

Time: [   ]   Case Number: [   ]   Investigator: [   ]

Weather:	**Death Scene Area:**	**State of Decomposition:**	**Exposure:**
☐ Sunny	☐ Forest	☐ Fresh	☐ Open Air
☐ Cloudy	☐ Field	☐ Bloat, Full	☐ Buried
☐ Partly Cloudy	☐ Pasture	☐ Bloat, Partial	Depth (inches) [ ]
☐ Rain	☐ Brush	☐ Bloat, Minor	☐ Surface
☐ Sleet	☐ Roadside	☐ Active Decay	☐ Clothed, Fully
☐ Snow	☐ Barren Area	☐ Advanced Decay	☐ Clothed, Partial
☐ Fog	☐ Closed Building	☐ Skeletonization	☐ Nude
☐ Other (Explain in Narr)	☐ Open Building	☐ Mummification	☐ Chemicals
Aquatic Habitat:	☐ Vacant Lot	☐ Dismemberment	☐ Gases
☐ Pond	☐ Trash Container	☐ Disembowelment	☐ Scavengers
☐ Lake	☐ Pavement	☐ Saponification	☐ Other (Explain in Narr)
☐ Creek	☐ Other (Explain in Narr)	☐ Other (Explain in Narr)	

☐ River

Scene Temperature:

☐ Swamp

Ambient Temp [   ]   Water (if aquat.) [   ]

☐ Canal

Body Surface [   ]   **Other Heat Factors:**

☐ Ditch

Ground Surface [   ]   ☐ Air Conditioning On

☐ Fresh Water

Ground/Body [   ]   ☐ Heat On

☐ Salt Water

Maggot Mass [   ]   ☐ Fan On

☐ Brackish Water

Other Factors Affecting Remains [   ]

Artifacts: indicate on drawing and list here. [   ]

Signature [   ]   Page [   ]

Inventory Control Number | Images Taken

Evidence Collected

#		#		#		#	
1		11		1		11	
2		12		2		12	
3		13		3		13	
4		14		4		14	
5		15		5		15	
6		16		6		16	
7		17		7		17	
8		18		8		18	
9		19		9		19	
10		20		10		20	

Photo Images

Narrative

Signature   Supervisor's Signature

Page

Laboratory Submission
Request

Report Classification [   ]   Case Number [   ]

Date/Time [   ]   Agency [   ]   Investigator [   ]

Victim's Name [   ]   Victim's Address [   ]

Type of Case [   ]   Inventory Control Number [   ]

Item No.	Description of Item	Type of Test or Examination Requested	Returned to Agency Date

Note: Item numbers above should be the same as those on the report form and the inventory form. Items from separate locations or recovered under a different case number should be listed on separate lab submission sheets. Describe below pertinent information that could help in examination or testing (required).

Case Info

Submitting Officer	Lab Person Receiving	Date/Time
Signature	Signature	Page

Dear Dr. Williams,

Please examine the enclosed exhibits to determine a PMI for our victim. He was discovered on June 1, 0000, in a wooded area off Route 66 and 500 West, Yourtown, OK. I have also included our forensic entomology collection form along with specimens.

The exhibits listed on a laboratory submission request are submitted for your evaluation.

Sincerely,

CSI _____

Yourtown, Oklahoma, Police Department

Notes

Chapter

Additional Practice with Your Camera

Goal: The goal of this exercise is to get additional practice with the camera. The camera is a very important tool for the CSI because a camera can document a scene with more detail than a report, drawing, and notes combined. It is necessary to know the camera as well as you know your partner.

In this exercise you will work without a partner.

1. Take 10 photo images of each of the following:
   a. Various items and perspective shots outside with daylight and no flash
   b. Various items and perspective shots inside with flash
   c. Various items and perspective shots inside without flash

2. Take five photo images of each of the following:
   a. Various items with candlelight, no flash
   b. Various items with incandescent (light bulbs), no flash
   c. Various items with a flash as the main light source
   d. Various items with a fluorescent light, no flash

3. Take five photo images of each of the following:
   a. Smooth surfaced objects (with or without flash)
   b. Rough surfaced objects (with or without flash)
   c. An object that is reflective, e.g., a CD jewel case. Note: It is important to be able to read the disk or cover inside the jewel case.
   d. Transparent objects with fluid in them. Milk, pop, beer, juice, etc.

4. Take three photo images of each of the following:
   a. Printed material, newspaper
   b. Printed material, magazine glossy paper
   c. Pictures from textbooks
   d. Items with LCD screens
   e. Cell telephone screen
   f. Television screen

List the images and record any unusual methods or techniques that you used that seemed to make a better image.

Name: _____ Date: _____
Print your photo images and turn them in with this listing sheet.

Image Description	Special Lighting, Tool, or Technique

Image Description	Special Lighting, Tool, or Technique

Image Description	Special Lighting, Tool, or Technique

Image Description	Special Lighting, Tool, or Technique

Notes

Chapter

Microscopy

Goal: The goal of this exercise is to learn and practice identifying hair samples.

In this exercise you will work without a partner.

The Scenario

The victim's body was discovered by a person getting into his car at an apartment complex located at 102 Sam Houston St., Yourtown, TX. The witness stated he saw the victim lying on the ground and called 911 from his cell phone. The police arrived and checked for vitals. The victim was dead. CSI Jordan collected trace samples from the victim. He was also able to obtain four images of a fourth sample. (All items have been submitted.)

This is a lab exercise. Examine 3 slides under a microscope designated by your instructor and the four images in Figure 21.1, Figure 21.2, Figure 21.3 and Figure 21.4. Figures 21.1 through Figures 21.4 are all the same sample. Samples 1, 2, and 3 are the slides, and Sample 4 is represented by the four images: 1.1, Figure 21.2, Figure 21.3 and Figure 21.4.

Complete the lab report for each item examined (samples 1 through 4). Make observations and draw conclusions referencing the following for each sample:

- Macroscopic features (what you see with the naked eye)
- Hair or fiber and justify your answer (microscopic features)
- Is the hair natural or dyed?
- Can DNA be recovered from each individual sample?
- What species is the hair from?
- What body region was the hair from?
- Can a racial ID be made?
- What are the hair characteristics?
- Was it shed/cut/broken/twisted/ripped/torn? (Look at both ends.)
- Make any recommendations for further testing (DNA, gas chromatography/mass spectrometry, burn/tensile strength testing, serology, drug testing, etc.)

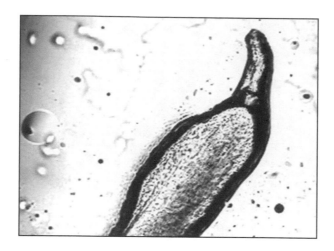

Figure 21.1
Sample 4

Figure 21.2
Sample 4

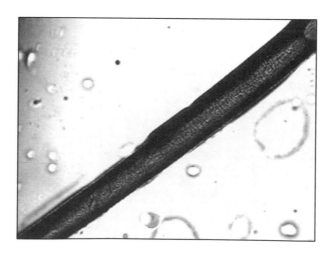

Figure 21.3
Sample 4

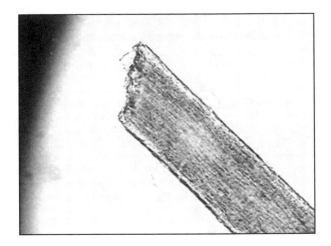

Figure 21.4.
Sample 4

Laboratory Submission Request
Forensic Science Laboratory

Date: 10.15.0000 Time 1344 hrs.	Case #: 0000-018	Case Type: Car Crash	Inventory #: I-0000-018
Location of Incident: **102 Sam Houston St., Yourtown, TX.**		Agency Name: **Texas State Police**	
Victim Name: **Andrew L. Wright**		Investigator: **Jordan**	

Item	Description of Item	Type of Test or Examination Requested	Returned to Agency: Date & Initial
1	Sample 1 from victim	Identify with as much information as is possible. Suggest additional tests as appropriate.	
2	Sample 2 from victim	Identify with as much information as is possible. Suggest additional tests as appropriate.	
3	Sample 3 from victim	Identify with as much information as is possible. Suggest additional tests as appropriate.	
4	Sample 4 – 4 images of a sample	Identify with as much information as is possible. Suggest additional tests as appropriate.	
	End		

Note: Item number corresponds to item number of evidence. If recovered at a different location, under a different case number (or supplementary number/letter), a separate submission should be used.

Describe any pertinent information that may aid in the examination and/or testing of this submission.
The four samples submited for examiation were recovered from the victim at the scene of a bludgeoning. Victim died of blunt force trauma. The weapon has not been recovered. Samples are suspected from the perpetratior due to the fact that the victim was bald and totally free from hair (medical condition). End.

Person Submitting (Printed)		Lab Personnel Receiving (Printed)	Date:
Jordan			Time:
Person Submitting (Signature)		Lab Personnel Receiving (Signature)	

Report of Laboratory Findings

Name:	Lab Section: Trace	Case Type:
Officer Name:	Date In:	Date Out:
Case Number: 0000-021	Inventory Control Number:	

Item	Describe item In Detail. Viscosity, Color, Etc.	Identity of Item or Match
Sample 1		
Sample 2		
Sample 3		
Sample 4 Figure 21.1		
Sample 4 Figure 21.2		
Sample 4 Figure 21.3		
Sample 4 Figure 21.4		

Returned to Agency By:	Lab Section: Trace	Case Type:
Officer Name:	Date Returned:	Officer Initials:

Notes

Chapter

Footwear Impressions

Goal: The goal of this exercise is to learn and practice methods of casting footwear impressions.

In this exercise you will work without a partner.

The Scenario

A burglary was reported at 31 Spooner St., Quahog, RI. Officer Joe Swanson, the uniformed officer taking the report, has discovered that the POE (point of entry) is the rear (east) entry door. Two other CSIs have processed the scene inside and did not recover any evidence; however, they did document the scene. After the CSI team left, Officer Swanson discovered a footwear impression in the flower garden just south of the door. The footwear impression was 13" north of the edge of the sidewalk and 10" from the base of the wall. The sidewalk is 42" wide at this point. The footwear impression appears to be quite large, perhaps a men's size 12 or 13. No one in the victim's family has a shoe size that large. (The victim's name is Peter Griffin. Peter is 5'8", 275 lbs. His shoe size is men's 8. He has a wife, Lois. Her shoe size is women's 8. They have three children, a boy, Chris, shoe size 9; girl, Meg, shoe size women's 5; and a toddler, Stewie. They also have a dog named Brian.) Since no one in the family wears that size shoe, Officer Swanson has called for a CSI to recover the footwear impression.

General Information

1. Weather outside is damp, foggy, and cool, 67°F.
2. FYI only: The victim states that his most valuable possessions were taken: 10 cases of beer and 22 years of *National Geographic* magazines.

Report Forms

1. Crime scene investigator's supplemental report. Case number: 0000-022-A. The classification is burglary.
2. Inventory sheet. Inventory control number: I-0000-022-A
3. Photo images
4. Evidence (the casting)

Procedure

1. Process the scene.

2. Take measurements of the footwear impression.

3. Photo image the footwear impression. Be sure to use a scale. Use oblique lighting (light source at 45 degrees to the footwear impression, Fig. 22.1).

4. Cast the footwear impression using the plaster provided.

5. After the casting has hardened, use a permanent marker and mark the opposite side of the impression with your name, date, location recovered, and case number.

6. Photo image the casting using oblique light. Note: When photo imaging the casting, photograph with scale only.

7. Note: Since no one is in custody, there is no footwear (shoe) to compare to your casting. A lab submission for analysis is not required until such time as there is a shoe to compare to the casting. It will be kept in inventory until you have a shoe to compare to the impression.

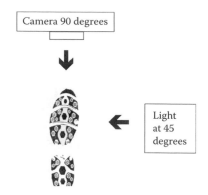

Figure 22.1
This drawing shows the type of lighting recommended for footwear impressions in dirt, sand, or mud.

Crime Scene Investigator's
Supplemental Report

Report Classification [   ]   Case Number [   ]

Date/Time [   ]   Type of Location [   ]   Agency [   ]   Investigator [   ]

Victim's Name [   ]   Victim's Address [   ]

Inventory Control Number [   ]   Images Taken [   ]

Evidence Collected				Photo Images			
1		11		1		11	
2		12		2		12	
3		13		3		13	
4		14		4		14	
5		15		5		15	
6		16		6		16	
7		17		7		17	
8		18		8		18	
9		19		9		19	
10		20		10		20	

Narrative:

Signature   Supervisor's Signature

Note: Start listing photo images on this report - if additional
space is needed use photo image continuation report.

Page [   ]

Narrative Continued: **Note: Do not print or use this page unless additional space is needed.**

Signature	Supervisor's Signature	Page

Inventory Sheet

	Case Number	
Date/Time	Agency	Investigator
Type of Case	Inventory Control Number	

Item No.	Quantity	Description of Items

Note: Item numbers above should be the same as those on the report form. Items recovered from separate locations or recovered under a different case number should be listed on separate lab submission sheets.
Describe below pertinent information that could help in examination or testing (required).

Case Info

Submitting Officer	Date/Time	
Signature		Page

Notes

Appendix A

Report Form Instructions: General

1. All reports must be written in technical style, not a creative writing style. Technical writing is documenting the facts in words. Sentences such as, "The billowing clouds cast their progeny of drops onto the cascading cacophony of feral rocks lying in wait below," should not be used. "The rocks were wet with rain" states the facts.

2. When writing a narrative, always refer to yourself as RI (reporting investigator) or RCSI (reporting crime scene investigator). The first time you use RI you should place "(reporting investigator)" next to it in parentheses as shown to identify the abbreviation. From there forward, you may use RI to represent reporting investigator.

3. All boxes (fields) must be completed. No field should be left empty.

4. Each box or field must contain
    a. The information requested.
    b. If the information exists, but is not known, enter UNK.
    c. If the information does not exist, enter N/A.
    d. If the answer to the field's request is zero, enter NONE.

5. In addition to your name (printed), your signature or initials must appear on the report (whatever is called for on each individual report). Be sure to initial each page, even those pages that do not call for an initial or a signature.

6. Following the last entry in a narrative, list, or other open space, you must write the word END. You must then draw a *single* diagonal line *(from upper left to bottom right)* in the remaining blank area. This is done to prevent the later addition of information from a source other than the author.

7. All lines drawn must be straight—use a ruler. This includes crime scene drawings.

8. The narrative should begin with the following: *"Reporting investigator (RI) was assigned to a* [type of case] *located at* [address, city, and state]. *Upon arrival, RI signed the scene entry log and spoke with* [first officer or detective on scene—name him or her], *who advised* [one or two sentences describing what the officer had observed. Your observations should be written into the report, not into the responding officer's. *RI then proceeded to process the scene."* Next describe what you saw, what you processed, what you collected, how you collected it, and any other detailed observations of the scene. The narrative should tell the story. *Remember: Who, what, when, where, how, and why* must be answered in the narrative. There should be no six sentence narratives.

9. Take your time when writing your report. It is essential that your report be complete and accurate. The simplest report should take you about a half hour. Don't just jot something down. Once you have written your report, set it aside for a while and then go back to it. Reread it and make any appropriate additions and corrections. Do not write the assignments in class. This is a formal report which, in the real world, may go to court and affect the outcome of a capital case. (Life and death!)

10. When numbering pages, group them as to the type of report. For example, if the CSI report has the cover page (1), the narrative page (2), and a photo listing sheet (3), these are: page 1 of 3, page 2 of 3, and page 3 of 3. If there is an inventory sheet or a lab submission sheet, it is 1 of 1. If there are so many items that a second page is necessary, it is page 1 of 2 and page 2 of 2. If there is only one page, it is page 1 of 1.

11. There should be only one narrative and it should be located on either the investigator's report or the supplemental report (the main case report for that case number). The narrative should not be duplicated. When it is written on the main case report, all other narratives in the package should have a single line drawn from the upper left to the bottom right.

12. Some reports have two signature blocks. Sign it only once; the second block is for your supervisor's signature. When the supervisor has signed the report, it is officially filed.

13. Be specific and include details when writing a narrative. Remember: The questions who, what, when, where, how, and why should be answered in detail.

14. Do not repeat your narrative on additional reports. If there is additional information concerning that report or form, place only the new information in this narrative.

15. Never say in any area of the report "see other report." Write it again. A person reading a report may not have physical or legal access to the other report you are referring to.

16. If you make a mistake, do not erase or scratch it out. *Draw a single line through it,* initial the mistake, date it, and insert the correction.

Specific Reports

1. **Crime scene entry log**

    a. This report form is used for major cases such as homicide, suicide, sex offense scenes, and search warrants. It is not normally used for a simple burglary. Rule of thumb: If there is a scene perimeter (crime scene tape), then there is a crime scene entry log. This report is created and signed at the scene.

    b. You, as a CSI, *will never be the first person on the log sheet.* This space is for the scene security officer, usually the first responder or first uniformed officer on the scene. As a CSI, you are called to the scene by others.

    c. Page numbers are counted only for the crime scene entry log and begin with 1. The numbers do not continue from the main report or other documents.

    d. Following the last entry on the sheet, you must write the word END. Then you must draw a single diagonal line from upper left to bottom right in the remaining blank area. This is to prevent the later addition of individuals who were not actually signed in and out.

2. **Crime scene investigator's report**

    a. Most items on the report are self-explanatory.

    b. Lighting conditions require the type of light, i.e., daylight, incandescent, fluorescent, candle, not ambient.

    c. Weather conditions: Even if the crime scene is indoors, we want to know what it is like outdoors, i.e., sunny, cloudy, raining, snowing, etc.

    d. Ambient temperature is the existing temperature; it requires the numerical temperature at the crime scene. Remember to indicate Fahrenheit or Centigrade. Be consistent. Don't use both in the same report. Since most people reading the report will be civilians, it is recommended that you use Fahrenheit.

    e. Evidence collected.

    i. The inventory control number is associated with the case number. The assigned inventory control designation is followed by the case number, i.e., I-2008-001 (I is for inventory). If a second inventory control number is used, such as with a supplementary report, the inventory control number would be I-2008-001-A.

(This would then be associated with the supplemental case number, which is given an alphabetic identifier such as A.)

Original case number	0000-001	Primary scene
Inventory control number	I-0000-001	Primary scene
Supplemental report	0000-001-A	Secondary scene
Inventory control number	I-0000-001-A	Secondary scene

    ii. Remember that each piece of evidence recovered should have the inventory control number on it in addition to the item number. The item number should be consistent throughout your reports. If the gun is item 14, then it is always item 14 and associated with the same inventory control number.

   iii. All numbers need to be consistent in your reports. If an item is item 1 on the case report, it should be item 1 on the inventory sheet and should be referred to as item 1 in the narrative of your report.

   iv. Use one envelope or bag for each individual piece of evidence. Three shell casings, three evidence containers.

    v. The narrative: Follow the rules stated in this Appendix A Report Forms—General.

3. Crime scene investigator's supplemental report

   a. This report is used if you are processing a secondary site or if the report is the result of an addition to a report that has already been filed. For example, if a shooting report (scene) has been processed and you are required to go to a second location to recover a firearm or projectile, you will complete a supplemental report.

   b. If additional evidence is recovered and evidence has already been recovered and documented on the original report, then your inventory number is designated as an "A" inventory control number, i.e., if your case number for the supplemental report is 12345-A, then your inventory number is I-12345-A.

   c. Following the last entry of your photo listing or the last entry in a narrative, you must write the word END. You must then draw a single diagonal line from upper left to bottom right in the remaining blank area. This is to prevent the later addition of information from a source other than the author.

4. Inventory Sheet

   a. This sheet is used in addition to itemizing the evidence collected on the crime scene investigator's report and the supplemental report. This sheet follows the evidence into the evidence property room even if the evidence is not sent to the crime lab for analysis. Note: All items are placed on the inventory sheet even if only some items are being sent to the lab. *All evidence and property is logged on this sheet.*

   b. If evidence is recovered at a location different from the one specified on the case report assigned to this location, use a separate inventory sheet and number.

   c. Following the last entry of your inventory sheet, you must write the word END. You must then draw a single diagonal line from upper left to bottom right in the blank area remaining. This is to prevent the later addition of information from a source other than the author.

5. Vehicle Processing report

   a. This form is used when a vehicle is processed, recovered, or examined.

   b. Use this form even if the vehicle is a truck. The drawing is that of a passenger vehicle, but it may be used with any vehicle.

   c. Indicate artifacts on the drawings of the vehicle. Note: An artifact is something that does not belong, such as a bullet hole, crash damage or broken items, paint transfers, bumper sticker, etc.

   d. VIN is the vehicle identification number. On cars, it is located on the driver's side dashboard, visible from the outside of the vehicle.

    e.   City sticker: Record the city sticker number (if it exists). Some cities, towns, and other jurisdictions use these as a source of tax revenue.

    f.   Odometer: This field calls for the mileage registered on the odometer.

    g.   Following the last entry of your photo listing, narrative, or evidence list, you must write the word END. You must then draw a single diagonal line from upper left to bottom right in the remaining blank area. This is to prevent the later addition of information from a source other than the author.

6. Handgun report

    a.   Use a single diagonal line to cross out the area not used (revolver or semi-automatic).

    b.   If the handgun is a revolver, neatly draw the chambers in the cylinder.

    c.   Neatly label the chambers as L–live, S–spent, or E–empty.

    d.   Following the last entry of your notes, you must write the word END. You must then draw a single diagonal line from upper left to bottom right in the remaining blank area. This is to prevent the later addition of information from a source other than the author.

7. Long Gun report

    a.   Use a single diagonal line to cross out the area not used (rifle or shotgun).

    b.   Following the last entry of your notes, you must write the word END. You must then draw a single diagonal line from upper left to bottom right in the remaining blank area. This is to prevent the later addition of information from a source other than the author.

    c.   There should be only one narrative. It belongs on either the investigator's report or on the supplemental report. Do not duplicate the narrative. If it is written in one report, then all the other narratives in the package should have a single line drawn from the upper left to the bottom right.

8. Laboratory submission request

    a.   Be sure that the same inventory number used on the report is used on the lab request.

    b.   If the evidence to be submitted has two different numbers, one from an original report and one from a supplemental report, two lab requests must be completed.

    c.   The "Returned to Agency: Date & Initial" is a field completed by the *lab personnel* when returning the evidence to your agency. (You do not complete these boxes unless you are the lab person.)

    d.   Under "Describe any pertinent information," *you must write several sentences about the case.* Remember that the lab personnel do not get copies of your report. This data is important because it helps them understand the case they will be examining.

    e.   The fields under "Lab personnel receiving (printed and signature)" should be completed by the lab personnel when receiving the evidence at the lab. You do not complete these boxes unless you are the lab person receiving the evidence.

    f.   Following the last entry of your evidence and description of the case, you must write the word END. You must then draw a single diagonal line from upper left to bottom right in the blank area remaining. This is to prevent the later addition of information from a source other than the author.

9. Photo image continuation report

    a.   This is a *continuation sheet* for the crime scene investigator's report and the crime scene supplementary report. Start listing your photos on the reports. If there are too many, you will list them on this sheet. This sheet may also be used to list photos for an assignment that requires no other report form.

    b.   Following the last entry of your photos, you must write the word END. You must draw a single diagonal line from upper left to bottom right in the blank area remaining. This is to prevent the later addition of information from a source other than the author.

10. Evidence continuation form

    a.   This is a *continuation sheet* for the crime scene investigator's report and the crime scene supplementary report. Start listing your evidence on the report, and if there are too many items, list them on this sheet.

b. Following the last entry of your evidence, you must write the word END. You must then draw a single diagonal line from upper left to bottom right in the blank area remaining. This is to prevent the later addition of information from a source other than the author.

11. Body diagram report

   a. Following the last entry of your photo images, narrative, and evidence collected, you must write the word END. You must then draw a single diagonal line from upper left to bottom right in the blank area remaining. This is to prevent the later addition of information from a source other than the author.

   b. You must insure that the case number and the investigator's name appear on each page.

   c. Use a ruler to draw lines.

   d. Indicate measurements of all wounds (size) and location (e.g., 15.5″ from the top of the head and 4.3″ from the left of center line). Note: Left and right are the subject's or the victim's left and right.

   e. Use inches as opposed to centimeters and millimeters. Most people reading your reports are not familiar with the metric system.

   f. There should be only one narrative. It belongs on either the investigator's report or on the supplemental report. Do not duplicate the narrative. Once it is written in one report, then all other narrative fields or boxes in the package should have a single line drawn from the upper left to the bottom right.

12. Skeletal body diagram report

   a. Following the last entry of your photo images, narrative, and evidence collected, you must write the word END. You must then draw a single diagonal line from upper left to bottom right in the blank area remaining. This is to prevent the later addition of information from a source other than the author.

   b. You must insure that the case number and the investigator's name appear on each page.

   c. Use a ruler to draw lines.

   d. Indicate measurements of all wounds (size) and location (e.g., 15.5″ from the top of the head and 4.3″ from the left of center line). Note: Left and right are the subject's or the victim's left and right.

   e. There should be only one narrative. It should be entered on either the investigator's report or on the supplemental report. Do not duplicate the narrative. Once it is written in one report, then all other narrative fields in the package should have a single line drawn from the upper left to the bottom right.

13. Crime scene drawing

   a. Should be drawn on graph paper (¼″ × ¼″) squares.

   b. Lines *must be drawn using a ruler.*

   c. Print neatly. This report, as with all of the reports, may be read by a judge, jury, prosecutor, and defense attorney.

   d. Identify items in the drawing.

   e. Show the dimensions of walls, doors, major items (measurements).

   f. The following must be placed on the drawing, *bottom right corner*:

   i. Your name.

   ii. The date.

   iii. The case number.

   iv. The location.

   v. "Drawing not to scale." This phrase is placed on all drawings even though they may be drawn to scale. This protects your testimony and the drawing from being thrown out due to an inadvertent mistake.

14. **Entomology collection form**

   a. Following the last entry of your photo images, narrative, and evidence collected, you must write the word END. You must then draw a single diagonal line (from upper left to bottom right) in the blank area remaining. This is to prevent the later addition of information from a source other than the author.

   b. Use a ruler to draw lines.

   c. Draw a single diagonal line in blocks asking for diagrams that do not apply.

   d. Use an "X" to cross out parts of the body that are missing.

   e. Indicate measurements of all wounds (size) and location (e.g., 15.5″ from the top of the head and 4.3″ from the left of center line). Note: Left and right are the subject's or the victim's left and right.

   f. If wounds are not discernable, indicate so in the narrative.

   g. There should be only one narrative. It belongs on either the investigator's report or on the supplemental report. If the only report to be completed is the entomological collection form, the narrative should be placed on this report.

Appendix B

Glossary

Abrasion	Injury caused by scraping off superficial skin due to friction against a rough surface
Active decay	The phase of decomposition following bloat that is characterized by maggot activity and a decrease in body weight
ADD	Accumulated degree days
ADH	Accumulated degree hours
Adiopocere	Waxy substance consisting of salts and fatty acids formed from decomposing tissue, especially in moist habitats
Advanced decay	The phase of decomposition following active decay that is characterized by beetle activity
Algor mortis	The lowering of body temperature—after death
Ambient temperature	The average air temperature around a given site; also, the fluctuating levels of heat in the air
Antemortem	Before death
Anthropologist	Study of human characteristics
Aperture	The opening of the lens on an SLR digital camera or a film camera that allows light to create the image on film or the image on the chip of a digital camera
Artifact	Anything that does not belong
ASA	Designates the speed of film or its sensitivity to light
Assault rifle	A weapon where ammunition is fed from a magazine
Automatic weapon	A firearm that continues to fire as long as the trigger is depressed and ammunition is available
Autopsy	Medical procedure, dissecting the cadaver to discover information of the death
Back spatter	Blood directed back toward the source of energy; often associated with entrance gunshot wounds
Ballistics	A branch of physics that deals with the flight of projectiles
Bloodstain	Transfer resulting when liquid blood comes into contact with a surface or a moist or wet surface comes into contact with dried blood
Blount force trauma	Injury sustained from a blunt object, i.e., baseball bat

Blow fly	Fly of the family Calliphoridae, also known as a bottle fly
Blowback	Blowing back of blood and other tissue onto a firearm or shooter from a near-contact or contact shot. This also refers to the mechanism in auto and semi-automatic weapons of the breechblock being forced to the rear, extracting and ejecting a shell casing
Bolt face signatures	Firing pin impressions and breechblock markings
Bubble ring	Ring produced when blood containing air bubbles dries and retains the bubble configuration as a dry outline
Bullet	The part of the cartridge that is expelled out the barrel of the gun (see Projectile)
Bullet wipe	A marginal abrasion may be overlaid by a gray ring of lubricant or metal from the bullet surface that has been wiped onto the skin. This may be found on any surface the bullet passes through
Caliber	Measurement associated with the diameter of a rifle and/or pistol bullet
Carbon monoxide	Gas; CO; non-breathable; used in suicides; produces a cherry pink tinge to skin
Cartridge	Includes the bullet, shell casing, primer, and powder
Cartridge head stamps	The base of a cartridge and shot shell bears information such as the vendor of the ammunition (abbreviated F for Federal, Rem for Remington, WIN for Winchester, and the gauge or caliber
Castoff pattern	Bloodstain pattern created when blood is released or thrown from a blood-bearing object in motion
Center fire cartridge	A cartridge in which the primer compound is contained in a centrally positioned primer cap
Choke	Constriction in the muzzle of a shotgun intended to concentrate the shot pattern
Class characteristics for firearms	Includes the caliber, shape, and location of firing pin as well as the size and shape of the extractor port; evidence that is not considered unique
Concentric cracks	Fractures that appear to circle around the point of impact
Conchoidal lines	Stress marks shaped like arches that are perpendicular to one glass surface and curved nearly parallel to the opposite surface; the perpendicular surface faces the side where the crack originated
Contact wound	Produced by the weapon in contact or within a fraction of an inch from the skin when discharged
Contusion	Bruise or leakage of blood from damaged blood vessels into tissue
Contusion ring	A marginal abrasion on the skin consisting of a circular or elliptical defect in the skin where a distant gunshot wound has entered
Coroner	Public officer charged with determining manner and cause of death; an elected position
Defense wounds	Wounds received by victim in attempting to ward off an attack
Digital camera	Camera that uses a digital media instead of film to record images
Directionality	The direction the blood was traveling when it impacted the target surface; can be determined by the geometric shape of the bloodstain pattern

Directionality angle	Angle between the long axis of a bloodstain and the line on the plane of the target surface that represents zero degrees
Drip pattern	Bloodstain pattern resulting from blood dripping into blood
Ejector	Device in an automatic or semiautomatic firearm that wrests the expended cartridge from the extractor and ejects it
Entomology	Study of insects
Exsanguination	Death after a significant amount of blood is lost
Film	Acetate based media that is sensitive to light and can be printed to an image
Film camera	Camera that uses safety film to record images; various sizes with 35 mm most popular—also 120″ which accommodates a number of formats and 4″ × 5″ sheet
Flash	A device that produces light at 5500 K (Kelvin)
Flow pattern	Change in the shape and direction of a wet bloodstain due to the influence of gravity or movement
Forcing cone	Flaring at the breech end of the barrel or a revolver that guides the bullet into firing
Forensic	Pertaining to legal
Forensic entomology	The study of insects and related arthropods from a legal aspect
Forward spatter	Blood that travels in the same direction as the source of energy or force
Full metal jacket	A bullet consisting of a lead core covered with a brass jacket over the nose and side of the bullet
Gauge	Measurement associated with the diameter of a shotgun shell
Hollow point bullet	A bullet where the nose of the bullet is drilled out allowing for a mushroom effect upon contact
Homicide	Deliberate taking of another's life
Imaging	Photographing using digital camera and digital media
Impact spatter	Bloodstain pattern created when blood receives a blow or force resulting in the random dispersion of smaller drops
Incised wound	Wound made by a sharp object, i.e., knife
ISO	Designates the speed of film or its sensitivity to light
KAA	A fluid composed of ethanol, glacial acetic acid, and kerosene used to preserve larvae
Kastle-Meyer Test	Presumptive blood test
Livor mortis	Pooling of the blood to the lowest part of the body by gravity—after death
Low velocity impact spatter	Bloodstains produced when the source is subjected to low velocity force
Macro photography	Close-up photography
Maggot mass	The collective, closely packed mass of fly larvae occurring in decomposing carrion
Manner of death	Natural, suicide, homicide, and accidental
Medical examiner	Public officer charged with determining manner and cause of death, an appointed position; a medical doctor specializing in forensic pathology

Medico-legal entomology	Medical entomology from a legal aspect
Medium velocity impact spatter	Spatter pattern when blood has been subjected to medium force; blood spatters produced in this manner are usually 1 to 3 mm in diameter; a beating typically causes this kind of spatter
Micro photography	Extreme close-up or microscopic photography
Migrating maggots	Third instar post feeding maggots that leave the corpse in order to pupate
Misting	Blood reduced to a fine spray as the result of some kind of force or energy
Mummification	Drying, shrinking and hardening of flesh, after death, due to extreme hydration
NA	Not applicable (the item does not exist)
Ninhydrin	Method of recovering latent fingerprints from dry paper and paper products
Perspective	Use of one item to show size and location relative to others
Petechia	Rupturing of small blood vessels in the eyes and eyelids—small reddish dots
Point of origin of convergence	A point or area to which a bloodstain pattern can be projected on a surface; determined by tracing the long axis of a well-defined bloodstain pattern back to a point of convergence
Postmortem	After death
Postmortem interval	Time between death and discovery of the body
Presumptive blood test	Test for the presence of blood—does not differentiate between human and nonhuman
Primer	Pressure-sensitive explosive that ignites the powder in a cartridge
Projectile	The part of the cartridge that is expelled out the barrel of the gun (see Bullet)
Pupation	To change form into a pupa in the process of transferring from larval stage to adult insect
Revolver	A handgun that holds cartridges in a cylinder; commonly referred to as a "wheel" gun
Rifling	Lands and groves in a barrel used to add stability to a bullet when fired
Rigor mortis	The stiffening of the muscles and tissue after death
Rim fire cartridge	A cartridge in which the primer compound is placed within the rolled rim of the casing. The firing pin strikes the rim of the cartridge
Scale	A ruler, usually 6″, used to show size when imaging
Scallop pattern	Bloodstain produced by a single drop characterized by a wave-like scalloped edge
Semi-automatic weapon	Firearm that fires and reloads itself before firing another shot
Semi-jacketed bullet	A bullet consisting of a lead core covered with a thin jacket of brass over the side of the bullet
Sharp force trauma	Injury sustained due to being cut or stabbed with a sharp object, i.e., a knife
Shot number	Number and size of pellets in a shotgun shell
Shutter speed	The amount of time that the shutter opens to allow light to strike the film in a film camera

Signature	A killer's psychological calling card left at each crime scene across a spectrum of several murders. Characteristics that separate or distinguish one murder from all others
Skid marks	Applied to marks near the nose of the bullet caused by contact with the forcing cone within the barrel
Slave	A secondary flash or strobe that fires when it sees the flash from the primary flash or strobe
Soft point bullets	Semi-jacketed bullets in which a soft metal plug has been inserted into the nose of the bullet
Spatter, blood	Dispersion of small blood droplets due to the forceful projection of blood
Stippling	Depositing of fragments of powder into the skin as the result of a gunshot wound of relatively close range; also called powder tattooing
Stringing	The use of string to plot the path of a projectile
Strobe	A device that produces light at 5500 K (Kelvin)
Suicide	Deliberate taking of one's own life
Toxicology	Study of toxins, poisons
Trace evidence	Physical evidence in very small quantities
Transfer pattern	Contact bloodstain created when bloody surface contacts a second surface and leaves a mirror image or a recognizable portion of the original surface pattern
Triangulation	Every item of evidence is measured from two fixed points
Twist	The direction of the rifling; such as right twist (Smith and Wesson) or left twist (Colt)
UNK	Unknown (the item exists, but is not known)
Wad (or wadding) found in shotgun shells	Cardboard, fiber, or plastic disk found in shot shells; may be placed between the powder and the shot or over the shot
Wave castoff	Small blood droplet from a parent drop caused by the wave-like action of the liquid when it strikes a surface at an angle smaller than 90 degrees
Wet particle method	Method of recovering latent fingerprints from wet paper or paper products

Appendix C

Scales

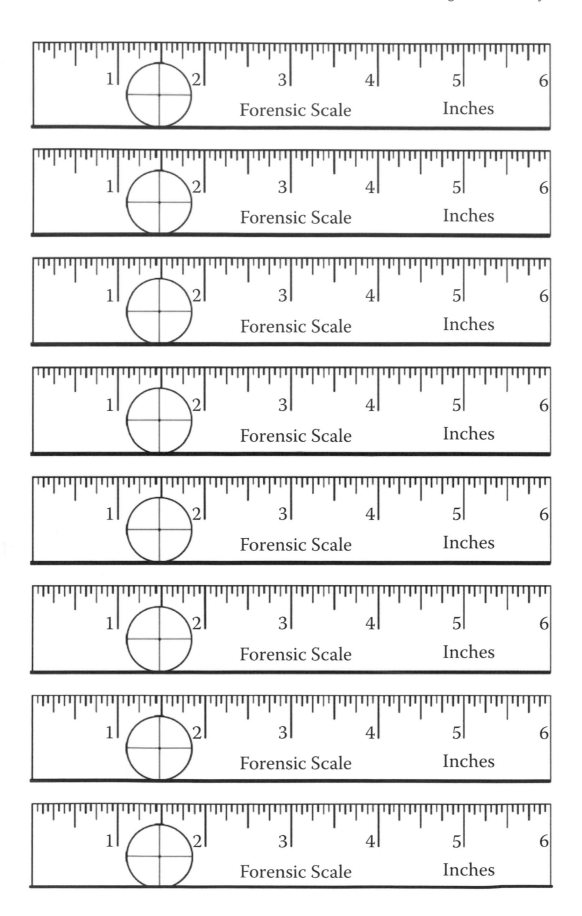

Appendix D

Tent Cards

1	**2**	**3**

4	5	6

7	8	9

10	11	12

13	14	15

16	**17**	**18**

192021

22	23	24

Photo ID and North Card

PHOTO I.D. CARD

Case Number:

Date / Time:

Forensic Photographer:

R   G   B   C   M   Y

Appendix F

How to Print Small Images

How to print wallet size pictures for lab submissions using Microsoft XP operating system

1. Place all images to print in one folder.
2. Open the folder.
3. On the top bar of the screen click "view".
4. Under view click "thumbnails".
5. On left of screen, under "picture tasks" click "print pictures".
6. A dialog box will open, "Welcome to the Printing Wizard", click "next".
7. Click "select all" or insure that the boxes next to the images have a check in them.
8. Click "next", this will open a dialog box, "printing preferences", click "next".
9. Go to "available layouts. Arrow down to wallet size. Click "3×5". This will generate a preview—four images per page.
10. Click "Next" and it will print.
11. Click "Finish".

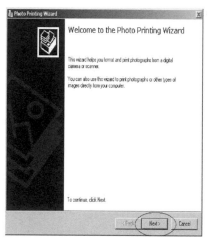

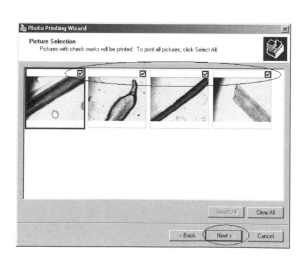

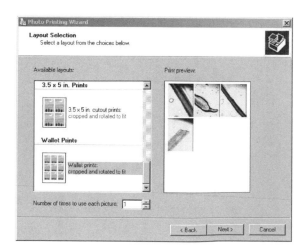

Appendix G

Extra forms

Crime Scene
Investigator's Report

Report Classification [   ] Case Number [   ]

Date/Time [   ] Type of Location [   ] Agency [   ] Investigator [   ]

Victim's Name [   ] Victim's Address [   ]

Injuries [   ] Taken for Treatment [   ] Victim Rape Kit [   ] Suspect in Custody [   ]

Suspect Rape Kit [   ] Weapon [   ] Gunshot Residue [   ] Gun Sheet [   ]

Weather [   ] Inside Temperature [   ] Outside Temperature [   ] Crime Scene Drawing [   ]

Alcohol [   ] Drugs [   ] Lighting Conditions [   ]

Vehicle [   ] Make [   ] Model [   ] Year [   ] Color [   ]

Vehicle Sheet [   ] License Plate [   ] License Plate State [   ]

Other Distinguishing Characteristics [   ]

Inventory Control Number [   ] Images Taken [   ]

Evidence Collected				Photo Images			
1		23		1		23	
2		24		2		24	
3		25		3		25	
4		26		4		26	
5		27		5		27	
6		28		6		28	
7		29		7		29	
8		30		8		30	
9		31		9		31	
10		32		10		32	
11		33		11		33	
12		34		12		34	
13		35		13		35	
14		36		14		36	
15		37		15		37	
16		38		16		38	
17		39		17		39	
18		40		18		40	
19		41		19		41	
20		42		20		42	
21		43		21		43	
22		44		22		44	

Note: Start listing photo images on this report - if additional space is needed use photo image continuation report.

Signature [   ] Page [   ]

Narrative:

Signature	Supervisor's Signature	Page

Crime Scene
Investigator's Report

Report Classification [   ]   Case Number [   ]

Date/Time [   ]   Type of Location [   ]   Agency [   ]   Investigator [   ]

Victim's Name [   ]   Victim's Address [   ]

Injuries [   ]   Taken for Treatment [   ]   Victim Rape Kit [   ]   Suspect in Custody [   ]

Suspect Rape Kit [   ]   Weapon [   ]   Gunshot Residue [   ]   Gun Sheet [   ]

Weather [   ]   Inside Temperature [   ]   Outside Temperature [   ]   Crime Scene Drawing [   ]

Alcohol [   ]   Drugs [   ]   Lighting Conditions [   ]

Vehicle [   ]   Make [   ]   Model [   ]   Year [   ]   Color [   ]

Vehicle Sheet [   ]   License Plate [   ]   License Plate State [   ]

Other Distinguishing Characteristics [   ]

Inventory Control Number [   ]   Images Taken [   ]

Evidence Collected				**Photo Images**			
1		23		1		23	
2		24		2		24	
3		25		3		25	
4		26		4		26	
5		27		5		27	
6		28		6		28	
7		29		7		29	
8		30		8		30	
9		31		9		31	
10		32		10		32	
11		33		11		33	
12		34		12		34	
13		35		13		35	
14		36		14		36	
15		37		15		37	
16		38		16		38	
17		39		17		39	
18		40		18		40	
19		41		19		41	
20		42		20		42	
21		43		21		43	
22		44		22		44	

Note: Start listing photo images on this report - if additional space is needed use photo image continuation report.

Signature [   ]   Page [   ]

Narrative:

Signature	Supervisor's Signature	Page

Crime Scene Investigator's
Supplemental Report

Report Classification [   ]   Case Number [   ]

Date/Time [   ]   Type of Location [   ]   Agency [   ]   Investigator [   ]

Victim's Name [   ]   Victim's Address [   ]

Inventory Control Number [   ]   Images Taken [   ]

	Evidence Collected					Photo Images	
1		11		1		11	
2		12		2		12	
3		13		3		13	
4		14		4		14	
5		15		5		15	
6		16		6		16	
7		17		7		17	
8		18		8		18	
9		19		9		19	
10		20		10		20	

Narrative:

Signature   Supervisor's Signature

Note: Start listing photo images on this report - if additional
space is needed use photo image continuation report.   Page [   ]

Narrative Continued: **Note: Do not print or use this page unless additional space is needed.**

Signature	Supervisor's Signature	Page

Crime Scene Investigator's
Supplemental Report

Report Classification [ ] Case Number [ ]

Date/Time [ ] Type of Location [ ] Agency [ ] Investigator [ ]

Victim's Name [ ] Victim's Address [ ]

Inventory Control Number [ ] Images Taken [ ]

Evidence Collected

1		11	
2		12	
3		13	
4		14	
5		15	
6		16	
7		17	
8		18	
9		19	
10		20	

Photo Images

1		11	
2		12	
3		13	
4		14	
5		15	
6		16	
7		17	
8		18	
9		19	
10		20	

Narrative:

Signature Supervisor's Signature

Note: Start listing photo images on this report - if additional space is needed use photo image continuation report. Page [ ]

Narrative Continued: Note: **Do not print or use this page unless additional space is needed.**

Signature	Supervisor's Signature	Page

Crime Scene
Entry Log

Report Classification [   ] Case Number [   ]

Location/Description [   ]

Type of Location [   ] Agency [   ] Log Officer [   ]

All persons entering this crime scene will sign in and out and state their purpose for entering.

Name & Title	Date/Time In	Date/Time Out	Reason for Entering

Signature of Log Officer

This report should not be typed. All entries
should be made by hand in black ink.   Page [   ]

Crime Scene
Entry Log

Report Classification [   ]   Case Number [   ]

Location/Description [   ]

Type of Location [   ]   Agency [   ]   Log Officer [   ]

All persons entering this crime scene will sign in and out and state their purpose for entering.

Name & Title	Date/Time In	Date/Time Out	Reason for Entering

Signature of Log Officer

This report should not be typed. All entries
should be made by hand in black ink.   Page [   ]

Inventory Sheet

Case Number _____

Date/Time _____ Agency _____ Investigator _____

Type of Case _____ Inventory Control Number _____

Item No.	Quantity	Description of Items

Note: Item numbers above should be the same as those on the report form. Items recovered from separate locations or recovered under a different case number should be listed on separate lab submission sheets.
Describe below pertinent information that could help in examination or testing (required).

Case Info

Submitting Officer	Date/Time
Signature	Page

Inventory Sheet

			Case Number	

Date/Time		Agency		Investigator	

Type of Case		Inventory Control Number	

Item No.	Quantity	Description of Items

Note: Item numbers above should be the same as those on the report form. Items recovered from separate locations or recovered under a different case number should be listed on separate lab submission sheets. Describe below pertinent information that could help in examination or testing (required).

Case Info

Submitting Officer	Date/Time
Signature	Page

Evidence Continuation
Report

Report Classification [   ] Case Number [   ]

Date/Time [   ] Type of Location [   ] Agency [   ] Investigator [   ]

Victim's Name [   ] Victim's Address [   ]

Inventory Control Number [   ]

Item Number	Description of Item

Signature   Supervisor's Signature   Page [   ]

Evidence Continuation
Report

Report Classification		Case Number	

Date/Time [   ]   Type of Location [   ]   Agency [   ]   Investigator [   ]

Victim's Name [   ]   Victim's Address [   ]

Inventory Control Number [   ]

Item Number	Description of Item

Signature	Supervisor's Signature	Page

Photo Image
Continuation Report

Report Classification [   ] Case Number [   ]

Date/Time [   ] Type of Location [   ] Agency [   ] Investigator [   ]

Victim's Name [   ] Victim's Address [   ]

Image Number   **Description of Image**

Signature   Supervisor's Signature   Page [   ]

Photo Image
Continuation Report

Report Classification		Case Number

Date/Time	Type of Location	Agency	Investigator

Victim's Name	Victim's Address

Image Number	Description of Image

Signature	Supervisor's Signature	Page

Vehicle Processing
Report

| Report Classification | | Case Number | |

| Date/Time | | Type of Location | | Agency | | Investigator | |

| Victim's Name | | Victim's Address | |

| Inventory Control Number | | Images Taken | |

Make	
Model	
Year	
Color	
Plate Number/State	
VIN	
Odometer	
Clock/Time	

Passenger Side   Top   Driver Side

| Windows | |

Draw lines and clearly identify artifacts on the vehicle. Number them and describe in narrative.

Climate Control		Blower/Fan		Keys in Ignition		Motor Running	
Radio		Exterior Temp		Interior Temp		Windows	
Vehicle Length		Front Bumper to Windshield		Front Window to Rear Window	
Vehicle Width		Rear Window to Rear Bumper		Lights	
Other Markings	

Evidence Collected

1		11		1		11	
2		12		2		12	
3		13		3		13	
4		14		4		14	
5		15		5		15	
6		16		6		16	
7		17		7		17	
8		18		8		18	
9		19		9		19	
10		20		10		20	

Photo Images

| Signature | Supervisor's Signature |

Note: Start listing photo images on this report - if additional space is needed use photo image continuation report.

| Page | |

Narrative Continued: **Note: Do not print or use this page unless additional space is needed.**

Signature	Supervisor's Signature	Page

Vehicle Processing
Report

Report Classification	Case Number

Date/Time	Type of Location	Agency	Investigator

Victim's Name   Victim's Address

Inventory Control Number   Images Taken

Make

Model

Year

Color

Plate Number/State

VIN

Odometer

Clock/Time

Passenger Side   Top   Driver Side

Windows

Draw lines and clearly identify artifacts on the vehicle. Number them and describe in narrative.

Climate Control   Blower/Fan   Keys in Ignition   Motor Running

Radio   Exterior Temp   Interior Temp   Windows

Vehicle Length   Front Bumper   Front Window to Rear Window
                      to Windshield

Vehicle Width   Rear Window to Rear Bumper   Lights

Other Markings

Evidence Collected   ## Photo Images

#		#		#		#	
1		11		1		11	
2		12		2		12	
3		13		3		13	
4		14		4		14	
5		15		5		15	
6		16		6		16	
7		17		7		17	
8		18		8		18	
9		19		9		19	
10		20		10		20	

Signature	Supervisor's Signature

Note: Start listing photo images on this report - if additional space is needed use photo image continuation report.

Page

Narrative Continued: **Note: Do not print or use this page unless additional space is needed.**

Signature	Supervisor's Signature	Page

Handgun Report

Report Classification [　　　　　　　　　　　] Case Number [　　　]

Date/Time [　　　] Type of Location [　　　] Agency [　　　] Investigator [　　　]

Victim's Name [　　　] Victim's Address [　　　]

Revolver

Make [　　　] Model [　　　] Finish [　　　] Serial Number [　　　]

Caliber [　　　] Sights [　　　] Chambers [　　　] Cocked [　　　] Rotation [　　　]

Ammunition Manufacturer [　　　] Photographed [　　　] Other Marks [　　　]

L=Live, S=Spent, E=Empty   **Label and/or Draw Chambers**

Draw in Custom

Semi-Automatic

Make [　　　] Model [　　　] Finish [　　　] Serial Number [　　　]

Caliber [　　　] Sights [　　　] Chambers [　　　] Cocked [　　　] Photographed [　　　]

Safety [　　　] Round in Chamber [　　　] Rounds in Magazine [　　　] Magazine Capacity [　　　]

Magazine in Weapon [　　　] Photographed [　　　] Other Marks [　　　]

Ammunition Manufacturer [　　　] Other Marks [　　　]

Narrative

Image Field

Signature   Supervisor's Signature

Draw single line through section not used.   Page [　　　]

Narrative Continued: **Note: Do not print or use this page unless additional space is needed.**

| Signature | Supervisor's Signature | Page |

Handgun Report

Report Classification [　　　　　　　　　　　] Case Number [　　　　]

Date/Time [　　] Type of Location [　　] Agency [　] Investigator [　　]

Victim's Name [　　　] Victim's Address [　　　　　]

Revolver

Make [　　] Model [　　] Finish [　　] Serial Number [　　]

Caliber [　　] Sights [　　] Chambers [　] Cocked [　] Rotation [　　]

Ammunition Manufacturer [　　] Photographed [　] Other Marks [　　]

L=Live, S=Spent, E=Empty   **Label and/or Draw Chambers**

Draw in Custom

Semi-Automatic

Make [　　] Model [　　] Finish [　　] Serial Number [　　]

Caliber [　　] Sights [　　] Chambers [　　] Cocked [　　] Photographed [　]

Safety [　] Round in Chamber [　] Rounds in Magazine [　] Magazine Capacity [　]

Magazine in Weapon [　] Photographed [　] Other Marks [　　　]

Ammunition Manufacturer [　] Other Marks [　　　]

Narrative

Image Field

Signature   Supervisor's Signature

Draw single line through section not used.   Page [　　]

Narrative Continued: Note: **Do not print or use this page unless additional space is needed.**

| Signature | Supervisor's Signature | Page |

Long Gun Report

Report Classification [ ] Case Number [ ]

Date/Time [ ] Type of Location [ ] Agency [ ] Investigator [ ]

Victim's Name [ ] Victim's Address [ ]

Shotgun

Make [ ] Model [ ] Finish [ ] Serial Number [ ]

Gauge [ ] Sights [ ] Chambers [ ] Cocked [ ] Cartridge in Chamber [ ]

Ammunition Manufacturer [ ] Photographed [.] Other Marks [ ]

Rifle

Make [ ] Model [ ] Finish [ ] Serial Number [ ]

Caliber [ ] Sights [ ] Ammo Fed [ ] Cocked [ ] Photographed [ ]

Safety [ ] Round in Chamber [ ] Rounds in Magazine [ ] Magazine Capacity [ ]

Magazine in Weapon [ ] Other Marks [ ]

Ammunition Manufacturer [ ] Action [ ]

Signature [ ] Supervisor's Signature [ ]

Page [ ]

Narrative

Signature   Supervisor's Signature

Page

Long Gun Report

Report Classification [   ]   Case Number [   ]

Date/Time [   ]   Type of Location [   ]   Agency [   ]   Investigator [   ]

Victim's Name [   ]   Victim's Address [   ]

Shotgun

Make [   ]   Model [   ]   Finish [   ]   Serial Number [   ]

Gauge [   ]   Sights [   ]   Chambers [   ]   Cocked [   ]   Cartridge in Chamber [   ]

Ammunition Manufacturer [   ]   Photographed [   ]   Other Marks [   ]

Rifle

Make [   ]   Model [   ]   Finish [   ]   Serial Number [   ]

Caliber [   ]   Sights [   ]   Ammo Fed [   ]   Cocked [   ]   Photographed [   ]

Safety [   ]   Round in Chamber [   ]   Rounds in Magazine [   ]   Magazine Capacity [   ]

Magazine in Weapon [   ]   Other Marks [   ]

Ammunition Manufacturer [   ]   Action [   ]

Signature [   ]   Supervisor's Signature

Page [   ]

Narrative

Signature   Supervisor's Signature

Page

Crime Scene Investigator's Forensic
Entomology Collection Form

Date: [   ] Case Type: [   ] Agency: [   ]

Time: [   ] Case Number: [   ] Investigator: [   ]

Weather:	**Death Scene Area:**	**State of Decomposition:**	**Exposure:**
☐ Sunny	☐ Forest	☐ Fresh	☐ Open Air
☐ Cloudy	☐ Field	☐ Bloat, Full	☐ Buried
☐ Partly Cloudy	☐ Pasture	☐ Bloat, Partial	Depth (inches) [ ]
☐ Rain	☐ Brush	☐ Bloat, Minor	☐ Surface
☐ Sleet	☐ Roadside	☐ Active Decay	☐ Clothed, Fully
☐ Snow	☐ Barren Area	☐ Advanced Decay	☐ Clothed, Partial
☐ Fog	☐ Closed Building	☐ Skeletonization	☐ Nude
☐ Other (Explain in Narr)	☐ Open Building	☐ Mummification	☐ Chemicals
Aquatic Habitat:	☐ Vacant Lot	☐ Dismemberment	☐ Gases
☐ Pond	☐ Trash Container	☐ Disembowelment	☐ Scavengers
☐ Lake	☐ Pavement	☐ Saponification	☐ Other (Explain in Narr)
☐ Creek	☐ Other (Explain in Narr)	☐ Other (Explain in Narr)	

☐ River	**Scene Temperature:**
☐ Swamp	Ambient Temp [ ] Water (if aquat.) [ ]
☐ Canal	Body Surface [ ] **Other Heat Factors:**
☐ Ditch	Ground Surface [ ] ☐ Air Conditioning On
☐ Fresh Water	Ground/Body [ ] ☐ Heat On
☐ Salt Water	Maggot Mass [ ] ☐ Fan On
☐ Brackish Water	

Other Factors Affecting Remains [   ]

Artifacts: indicate on drawing and list here. [   ]

Signature [   ]   Page [   ]

Inventory Control Number [   ]   Images Taken [   ]

	Evidence Collected				Photo Images		
1		11		1		11	
2		12		2		12	
3		13		3		13	
4		14		4		14	
5		15		5		15	
6		16		6		16	
7		17		7		17	
8		18		8		18	
9		19		9		19	
10		20		10		20	

Narrative

Signature   Supervisor's Signature

Page [   ]

Crime Scene Investigator's Forensic Entomology Collection Form

Date: [ ] Case Type: [ ] Agency: [ ]

Time: [ ] Case Number: [ ] Investigator: [ ]

Weather:	**Death Scene Area:**	**State of Decomposition:**	**Exposure:**
☐ Sunny	☐ Forest	☐ Fresh	☐ Open Air
☐ Cloudy	☐ Field	☐ Bloat, Full	☐ Buried
☐ Partly Cloudy	☐ Pasture	☐ Bloat, Partial	Depth (inches) [ ]
☐ Rain	☐ Brush	☐ Bloat, Minor	☐ Surface
☐ Sleet	☐ Roadside	☐ Active Decay	☐ Clothed, Fully
☐ Snow	☐ Barren Area	☐ Advanced Decay	☐ Clothed, Partial
☐ Fog	☐ Closed Building	☐ Skeletonization	☐ Nude
☐ Other (Explain in Narr)	☐ Open Building	☐ Mummification	☐ Chemicals
Aquatic Habitat:	☐ Vacant Lot	☐ Dismemberment	☐ Gases
☐ Pond	☐ Trash Container	☐ Disembowelment	☐ Scavengers
☐ Lake	☐ Pavement	☐ Saponification	☐ Other (Explain in Narr)
☐ Creek	☐ Other (Explain in Narr)	☐ Other (Explain in Narr)	

☐ River

Scene Temperature:

☐ Swamp Ambient Temp [ ] Water (if aquat.) [ ]

☐ Canal Body Surface [ ] **Other Heat Factors:**

☐ Ditch Ground Surface [ ] ☐ Air Conditioning On

☐ Fresh Water Ground/Body [ ] ☐ Heat On

☐ Salt Water Maggot Mass [ ] ☐ Fan On

☐ Brackish Water

Other Factors Affecting Remains [ ]

Artifacts: indicate on drawing and list here. [ ]

Signature [ ] Page [ ]

Inventory Control Number [   ]   Images Taken [   ]

Evidence Collected   **Photo Images**

1		11		1		11	
2		12		2		12	
3		13		3		13	
4		14		4		14	
5		15		5		15	
6		16		6		16	
7		17		7		17	
8		18		8		18	
9		19		9		19	
10		20		10		20	

Narrative
_____
_____
_____
_____
_____
_____
_____
_____
_____
_____
_____
_____
_____
_____
_____
_____
_____
_____
_____
_____
_____
_____
_____

Signature   Supervisor's Signature

Page [   ]

Body Diagram
Report

Case Classification [   ]   Case Number [   ]

Date/Time [   ]   Type of Location [   ]   Agency [   ]   Investigator [   ]

Victim's Name [   ]   Victim's Address [   ]

Weapon [   ]   Gunshot Residue [   ]   Gun Sheet [   ]   Rape Kit [   ]   Suspect in Custody [   ]

Alcohol [   ]   Drugs [   ]   Lighting Conditions [   ]

Inventory Control Number [   ]   Images Taken [   ]

Evidence Collected				Photo Images			
1		23		1		23	
2		24		2		24	
3		25		3		25	
4		26		4		26	
5		27		5		27	
6		28		6		28	
7		29		7		29	
8		30		8		30	
9		31		9		31	
10		32		10		32	
11		33		11		33	
12		34		12		34	
13		35		13		35	
14		36		14		36	
15		37		15		37	
16		38		16		38	
17		39		17		39	
18		40		18		40	
19		41		19		41	
20		42		20		42	
21		43		21		43	
22		44		22		44	

Narrative:

[   ]

Note: Start listing photo images on this report - if additional space is needed use photo image continuation report.

Signature   Supervisor's Signature   Page [   ]

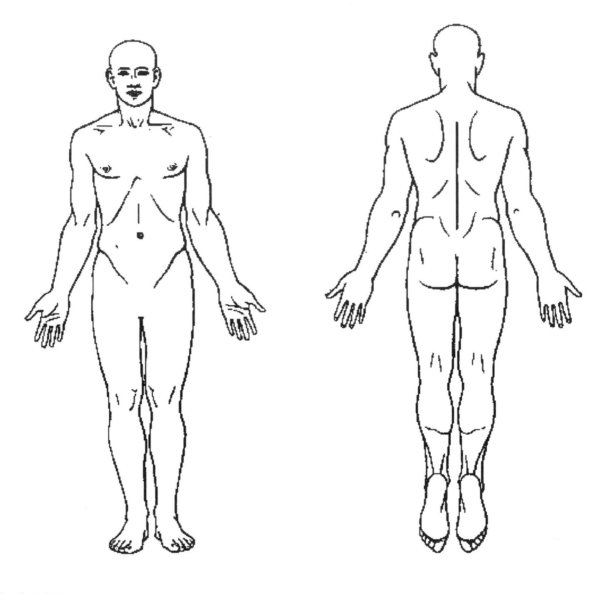

Identify artifacts.

Signature	Supervisor's Signature	Page

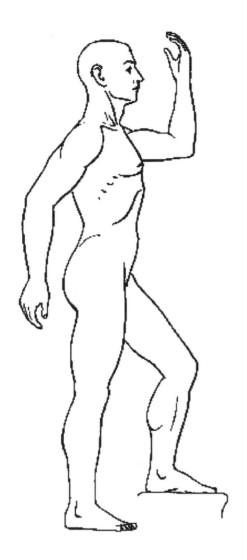
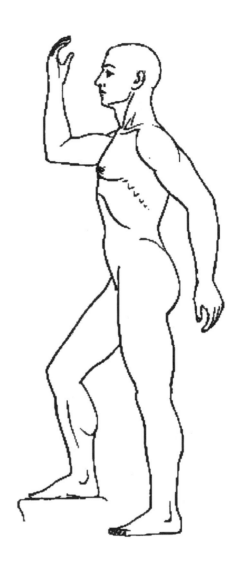

Identify artifacts:

_____
_____
_____
_____
_____
_____
_____

Signature	Supervisor's Signature	Page	

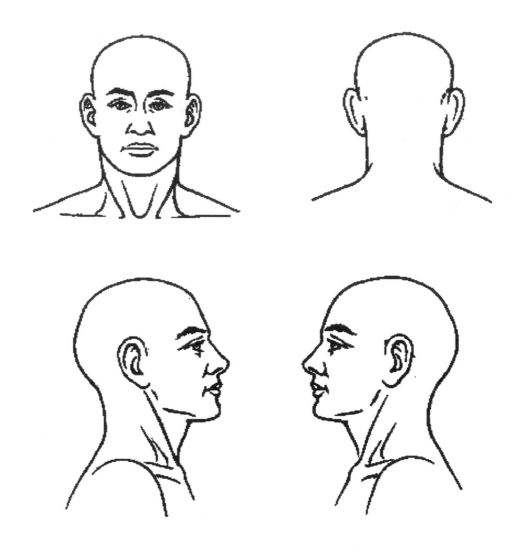

Identify artifacts.

Signature	Supervisor's Signature	Page	

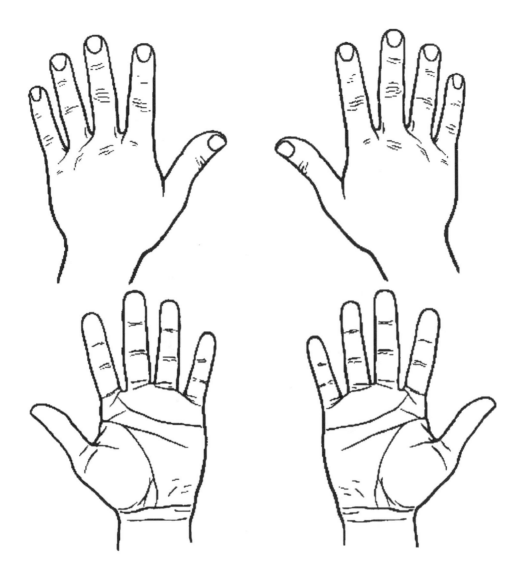

Identify artifacts

Signature	Supervisor's Signature	Page

Body Diagram
Report

Case Classification		Case Number	

Date/Time [ ] Type of Location [ ] Agency [ ] Investigator [ ]

Victim's Name [ ] Victim's Address [ ]

Weapon [ ] Gunshot Residue [ ] Gun Sheet [ ] Rape Kit [ ] Suspect in Custody [ ]

Alcohol [ ] Drugs [ ] Lighting Conditions [ ]

Inventory Control Number [ ] Images Taken [ ]

Evidence Collected				**Photo Images**			
1		23		1		23	
2		24		2		24	
3		25		3		25	
4		26		4		26	
5		27		5		27	
6		28		6		28	
7		29		7		29	
8		30		8		30	
9		31		9		31	
10		32		10		32	
11		33		11		33	
12		34		12		34	
13		35		13		35	
14		36		14		36	
15		37		15		37	
16		38		16		38	
17		39		17		39	
18		40		18		40	
19		41		19		41	
20		42		20		42	
21		43		21		43	
22		44		22		44	

Narrative:

Note: Start listing photo images on this report - if additional space is needed use photo image continuation report.

Signature   Supervisor's Signature   Page [ ]

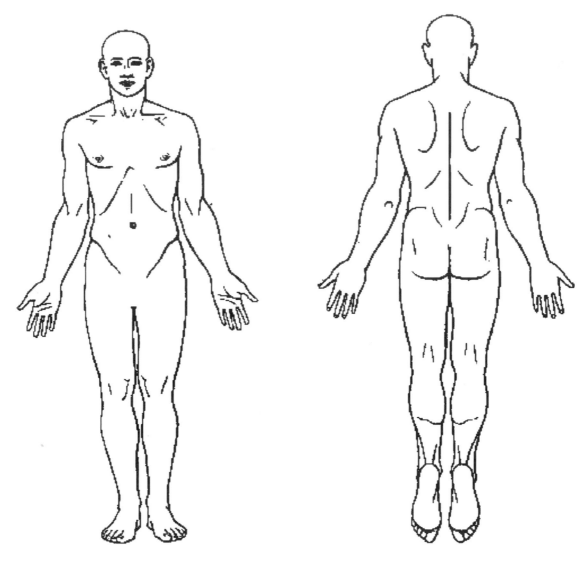

Identify artifacts.

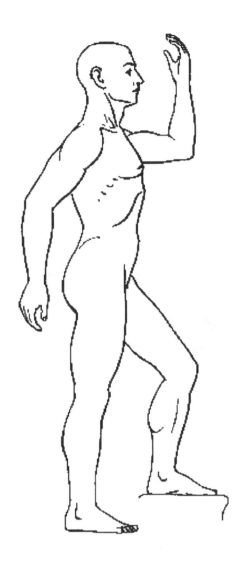 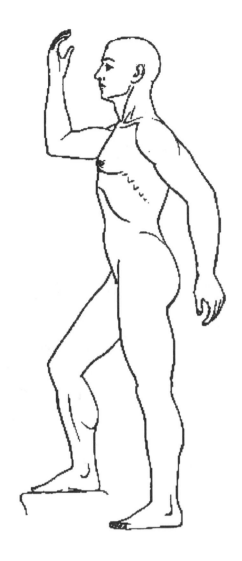

Identify artifacts:

Signature	Supervisor's Signature	Page	

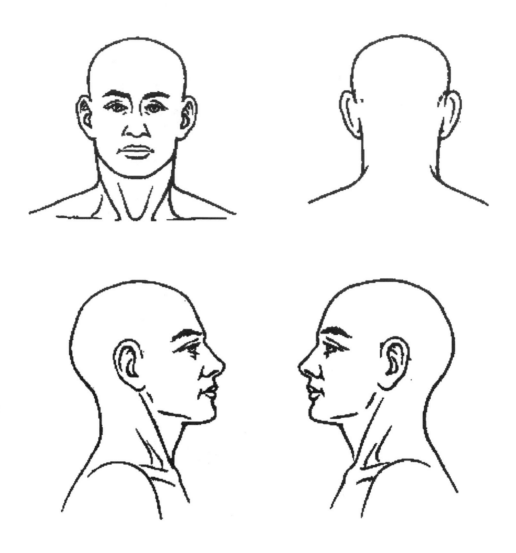

Identify artifacts.

Signature	Supervisor's Signature	Page	

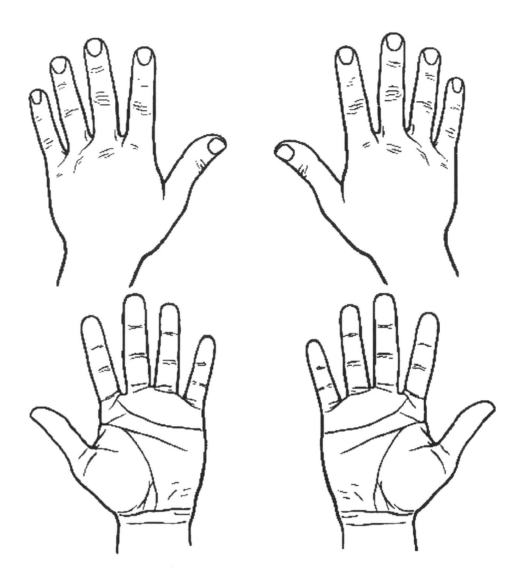

Identify artifacts

Skeletal Body
Diagram Report

Report Classification		Case Number	

Date/Time		Type of Location		Agency		Investigator	

Victim's Name		Victim's Address	

Weapon		Gunshot Residue		Gun Sheet		Rape Kit		Suspect in Custody	

Alcohol		Drugs		Lighting Conditions	

Inventory Control Number		Images Taken	

Evidence Collected				**Photo Images**			
1		23		1		23	
2		24		2		24	
3		25		3		25	
4		26		4		26	
5		27		5		27	
6		28		6		28	
7		29		7		29	
8		30		8		30	
9		31		9		31	
10		32		10		32	
11		33		11		33	
12		34		12		34	
13		35		13		35	
14		36		14		36	
15		37		15		37	
16		38		16		38	
17		39		17		39	
18		40		18		40	
19		41		19		41	
20		42		20		42	
21		43		21		43	
22		44		22		44	

Note: If evidence or photo images are already listed on another report, do not duplicate them on this report.

Narrative:

Note: Start listing photo images on this report - if additional space is needed use photo image continuation report.

Signature	Supervisor's Signature	Page	

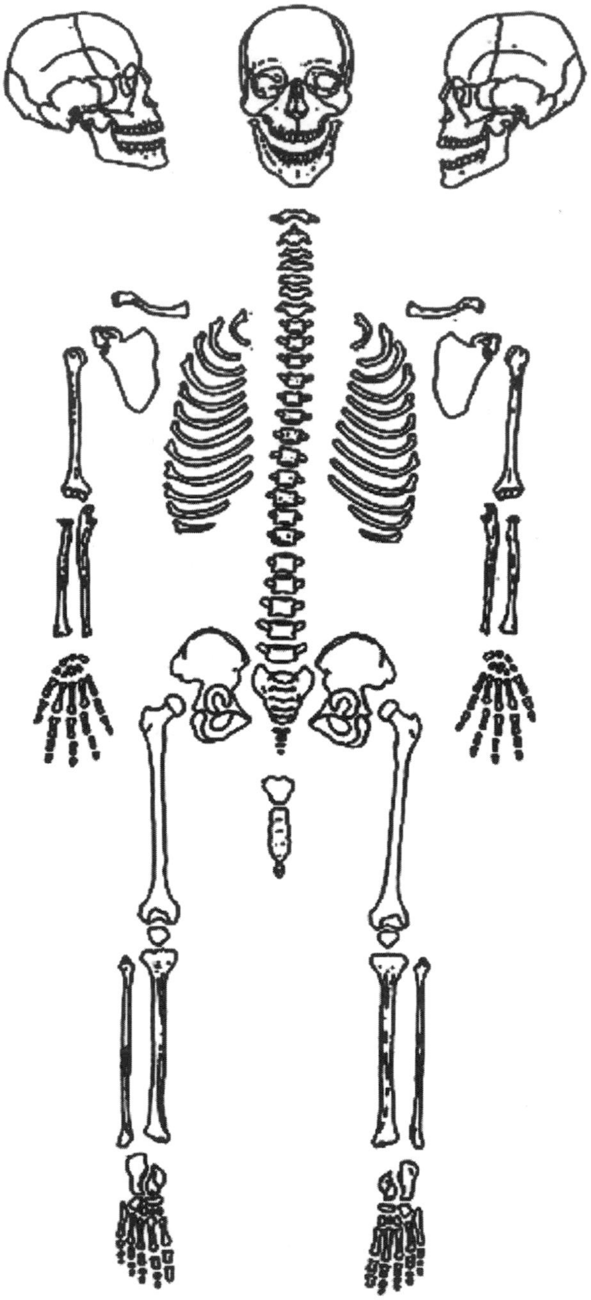

Artifacts:

Notes:

Draw line from artifact and identify.

Signature

Supervisor's Signature

Page

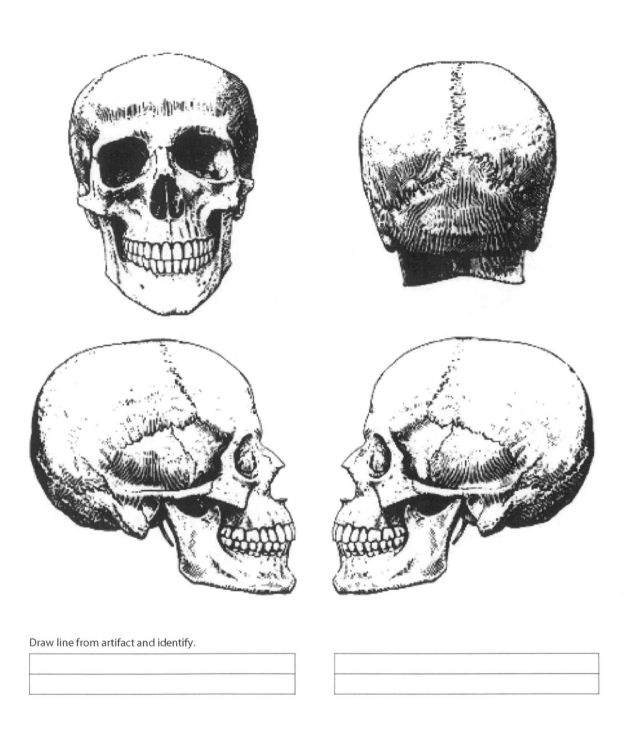

Draw line from artifact and identify.

Signature	Supervisor's Signature	Page	

Skeletal Body
Diagram Report

Report Classification [　] Case Number [　]

Date/Time [　] Type of Location [　] Agency [　] Investigator [　]

Victim's Name [　] Victim's Address [　]

Weapon [　] Gunshot Residue [　] Gun Sheet [　] Rape Kit [　] Suspect in Custody [　]

Alcohol [　] Drugs [　] Lighting Conditions [　]

Inventory Control Number [　] Images Taken [　]

Evidence Collected				Photo Images			
1		23		1		23	
2		24		2		24	
3		25		3		25	
4		26		4		26	
5		27		5		27	
6		28		6		28	
7		29		7		29	
8		30		8		30	
9		31		9		31	
10		32		10		32	
11		33		11		33	
12		34		12		34	
13		35		13		35	
14		36		14		36	
15		37		15		37	
16		38		16		38	
17		39		17		39	
18		40		18		40	
19		41		19		41	
20		42		20		42	
21		43		21		43	
22		44		22		44	

Note: If evidence or photo images are already listed on another report, do not duplicate them on this report.

Narrative:

Note: Start listing photo images on this report - if additional space is needed use photo image continuation report.

Signature　　Supervisor's Signature　　Page [　]

Artifacts: **Notes:**

Draw line from artifact and identify.

Signature	Supervisor's Signature

Page

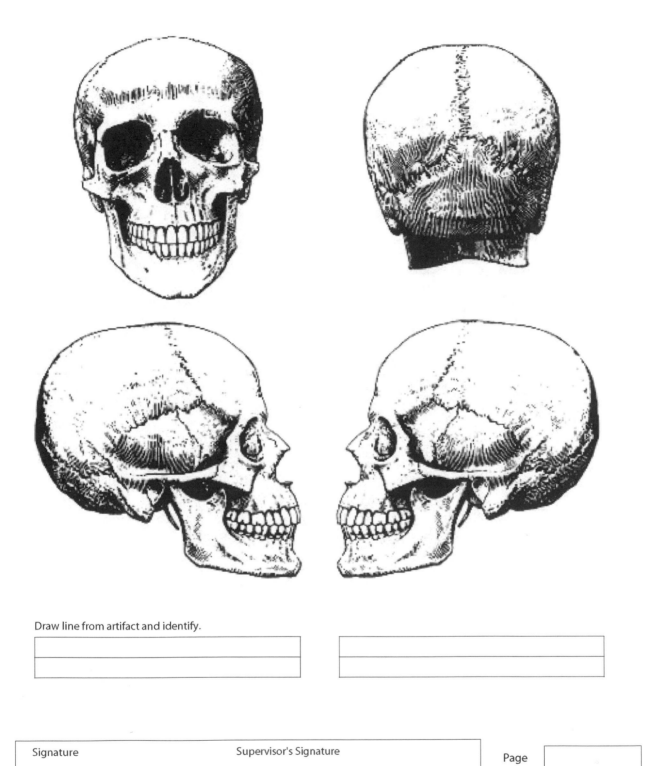

Draw line from artifact and identify.

Signature	Supervisor's Signature	Page	

Laboratory Submission
Request

Report Classification [   ]   Case Number [   ]

Date/Time [   ]   Agency [   ]   Investigator [   ]

Victim's Name [   ]   Victim's Address [   ]

Type of Case [   ]   Inventory Control Number [   ]

Item No.	Description of Item	Type of Test or Examination Requested	Returned to Agency Date

Note: Item numbers above should be the same as those on the report form and the inventory form. Items from separate locations or recovered under a different case number should be listed on separate lab submission sheets. Describe below pertinent information that could help in examination or testing (required).

Case Info		
Submitting Officer	Lab Person Receiving	Date/Time
Signature	Signature	Page

Laboratory Submission
Request

Report Classification [   ]   Case Number [   ]

Date/Time [   ]   Agency [   ]   Investigator [   ]

Victim's Name [   ]   Victim's Address [   ]

Type of Case [   ]   Inventory Control Number [   ]

Item No.	Description of Item	Type of Test or Examination Requested	Returned to Agency Date

Note: Item numbers above should be the same as those on the report form and the inventory form. Items from separate locations or recovered under a different case number should be listed on separate lab submission sheets. Describe below pertinent information that could help in examination or testing (required).

Case Info

Submitting Officer	Lab Person Receiving	Date/Time
Signature	Signature	Page

Appendix H

The Maggot Motel

1. Fold 8"x 8" foil:

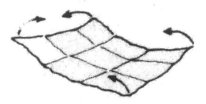

2. Into pouch:

3. Place a small piece of liver in pouch:

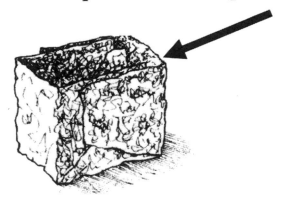

4. Place maggots into pouch on liver:

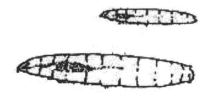

5. : Fold over foil and close pouch:

6. Place vermiculite into cup:

And place pouch with liver on top of vermiculite and cover:

7. Rear maggots to next stage, puparium:

8. Then to the final stage the fly. Observe and document.

Appendix I

Insect Sample Labels

Preserved ☐ Live ☐
Location:_____
Sample #:_____
Date_____Initials:_____

Preserved ☐ Live ☐
Location:_____
Sample #:_____
Date_____Initials:_____

Preserved ☐ Live ☐
Location:_____
Sample #:_____
Date_____Initials:_____

Preserved ☐ Live ☐
Location:_____
Sample #:_____
Date_____Initials:_____

Preserved ☐ Live ☐
Location:_____
Sample #:_____
Date_____Initials:_____

Preserved ☐ Live ☐
Location:_____
Sample #:_____
Date_____Initials:_____

Preserved ☐ Live ☐
Location:_____
Sample #:_____
Date_____Initials:_____

Preserved ☐ Live ☐
Location:_____
Sample #:_____
Date_____Initials:_____

Preserved ☐ Live ☐
Location:_____
Sample #:_____
Date_____Initials:_____

Preserved ☐ Live ☐
Location:_____
Sample #:_____
Date_____Initials:_____

Preserved ☐ Live ☐
Location:_____
Sample #:_____
Date_____Initials:_____

Preserved ☐ Live ☐
Location:_____
Sample #:_____
Date_____Initials:_____

Preserved ☐ Live ☐
Location:_____
Sample #:_____
Date_____Initials:_____

Preserved ☐ Live ☐
Location:_____
Sample #:_____
Date_____Initials:_____

Preserved ☐ Live ☐
Location:_____
Sample #:_____
Date_____Initials:_____

Preserved ☐ Live ☐
Location:_____
Sample #:_____
Date_____Initials:_____

Preserved ☐ Live ☐
Location:_____
Sample #:_____
Date_____Initials:_____

Preserved ☐ Live ☐
Location:_____
Sample #:_____
Date_____Initials:_____

Preserved ☐ Live ☐
Location:_____
Sample #:_____
Date_____Initials:_____

Preserved ☐ Live ☐
Location:_____
Sample #:_____
Date_____Initials:_____

Preserved ☐ Live ☐
Location:_____
Sample #:_____
Date_____Initials:_____

Preserved ☐ Live ☐
Location:_____
Sample #:_____
Date_____Initials:_____

Preserved ☐ Live ☐
Location:_____
Sample #:_____
Date_____Initials:_____

Preserved ☐ Live ☐
Location:_____
Sample #:_____
Date_____Initials:_____

Preserved ☐ Live ☐
Location:_____
Sample #:_____
Date_____Initials:_____

Preserved ☐ Live ☐
Location:_____
Sample #:_____
Date_____Initials:_____

Preserved ☐ Live ☐
Location:_____
Sample #:_____
Date_____Initials:_____

Preserved ☐ Live ☐
Location:_____
Sample #:_____
Date_____Initials:_____

Preserved ☐ Live ☐
Location:_____
Sample #:_____
Date_____Initials:_____

Preserved ☐ Live ☐
Location:_____
Sample #:_____
Date_____Initials:_____

Preserved ☐ Live ☐
Location:_____
Sample #:_____
Date_____Initials:_____

Preserved ☐ Live ☐
Location:_____
Sample #:_____
Date_____Initials:_____

Preserved ☐ Live ☐
Location:_____
Sample #:_____
Date_____Initials:_____

Preserved ☐ Live ☐
Location:_____
Sample #:_____
Date_____Initials:_____

Preserved ☐ Live ☐
Location:_____
Sample #:_____
Date_____Initials:_____

Preserved ☐ Live ☐
Location:_____
Sample #:_____
Date_____Initials:_____

Preserved ☐ Live ☐
Location:_____
Sample #:_____
Date_____Initials:_____

Preserved ☐ Live ☐
Location:_____
Sample #:_____
Date_____Initials:_____

Preserved ☐ Live ☐
Location:_____
Sample #:_____
Date_____Initials:_____

Preserved ☐ Live ☐
Location:_____
Sample #:_____
Date_____Initials:_____

Preserved ☐ Live ☐
Location:_____
Sample #:_____
Date_____Initials:_____

Preserved ☐ Live ☐
Location:_____
Sample #:_____
Date_____Initials:_____

Preserved ☐ Live ☐
Location:_____
Sample #:_____
Date_____Initials:_____

Preserved ☐ Live ☐
Location:_____
Sample #:_____
Date_____Initials:_____

Preserved ☐ Live ☐
Location:_____
Sample #:_____
Date_____Initials:_____

Preserved ☐ Live ☐
Location:_____
Sample #:_____
Date_____Initials:_____

Preserved ☐ Live ☐
Location:_____
Sample #:_____
Date_____Initials:_____

Preserved ☐ Live ☐
Location:_____
Sample #:_____
Date_____Initials:_____

Preserved ☐ Live ☐
Location:_____
Sample #:_____
Date_____Initials:_____

Preserved ☐ Live ☐
Location:_____
Sample #:_____
Date_____Initials:_____

Preserved ☐ Live ☐
Location:_____
Sample #:_____
Date_____Initials:_____

Preserved ☐ Live ☐
Location:_____
Sample #:_____
Date_____Initials:_____

Preserved ☐ Live ☐
Location:_____
Sample #:_____
Date_____Initials:_____

Preserved ☐ Live ☐
Location:_____
Sample #:_____
Date_____Initials:_____

Preserved ☐ Live ☐
Location:_____
Sample #:_____
Date_____Initials:_____

Preserved ☐ Live ☐
Location:_____
Sample #:_____
Date_____Initials:_____

Preserved ☐ Live ☐
Location:_____
Sample #:_____
Date_____Initials:_____

Preserved ☐ Live ☐
Location:_____
Sample #:_____
Date_____Initials:_____

Preserved ☐ Live ☐
Location:_____
Sample #:_____
Date_____Initials:_____

Preserved ☐ Live ☐
Location:_____
Sample #:_____
Date_____Initials:_____

Preserved ☐ Live ☐
Location:_____
Sample #:_____
Date_____Initials:_____

Preserved ☐ Live ☐
Location:_____
Sample #:_____
Date_____Initials:_____

Preserved ☐ Live ☐
Location:_____
Sample #:_____
Date_____Initials:_____

Preserved ☐ Live ☐
Location:_____
Sample #:_____
Date_____Initials:_____

Preserved ☐ Live ☐
Location:_____
Sample #:_____
Date_____Initials:_____

Preserved ☐ Live ☐
Location:_____
Sample #:_____
Date_____Initials:_____

Preserved ☐ Live ☐
Location:_____
Sample #:_____
Date_____Initials:_____

Preserved ☐ Live ☐
Location:_____
Sample #:_____
Date_____Initials:_____

Preserved ☐ Live ☐
Location:_____
Sample #:_____
Date_____Initials:_____

Preserved ☐ Live ☐
Location:_____
Sample #:_____
Date_____Initials:_____

Preserved ☐ Live ☐
Location:_____
Sample #:_____
Date_____Initials:_____

Preserved ☐ Live ☐
Location:_____
Sample #:_____
Date_____Initials:_____

Index